FISHING NORTHERN CANADA

for

LAKE TROUT, GRAYLING

and

ARCTIC CHAR

© 2015 by Duane S. Radford and Merrie Lyn Shickler

All rights reserved. No part of this work covered by the copyrights hereon may be reproduced or used in any form or by any means—graphic, electronic, or mechanical—without the prior written permission of the publisher, editors, and individual authors except for reviewers, who may quote brief passages. Any request for photocopying, recording, taping, or storage on information retrieval systems of any part of this work shall be directed in writing to the publisher.

Front Cover Photographs: David O'Farrell, Grizzly Creek Lodge owner and Adrienne Radford with a Toobally Lake, Yukon, lake trout (L); Dan Miguel, Frontier Fishing Lodge guide with a Stark River, NWT, Arctic grayling (top right); and Trevor Nowak, former head guide at Plummer's Arctic Lodge Tree River Lodge, with a Tree River Arctic char caught by co-editor Duane S. Radford on the Tree River, Nunavut (bottom right). Unless otherwise noted, photo credit for various photographs associated with the articles in this book belongs to the author noted in the titles for each chapter.

Published by North Country Press

ISBN: 978-0-692-32306-9

Editing and book design by Stacey Aaronson

Printed in the United States of America

FISHING NORTHERN CANADA
for
LAKE TROUT, GRAYLING
and
ARCTIC CHAR

*A Fisherman's Paradise in the
Land of the Midnight Sun*

Edited by
DUANE S. RADFORD
and
ROSS H. SHICKLER

NORTH COUNTRY PRESS

CONTENTS

INTRODUCTION *by Duane S. Radford*	1
DEDICATION	3
1. HOMAGE	
A Tribute to Lloyd Bull *by Mark Anderson*	5
2. NORTH OF SIXTY	
by Duane S. Radford and Ross H. Shickler	9
Geography	11
Angling Regulations	15
Recreational Fishing Surveys	19
Gearing Up for a North of Sixty Fishing Trip	20
Fishing Lodges	24
Fish ID & Biology 101	29
Climate Change	35
3. ARCTIC GRAYLING: A FLY-FISHING PRIMER	
by Duane S. Radford	39
4. NORTHWEST TERRITORIES (NWT)	47
Following the Ice North: Planning a Journey in the Northwest Territories (NWT) and Nunavut *by Chris Hanks*	49
Plummer's Arctic Lodges: Great Bear Lake Lodge *by Duane S. Radford*	57
Frontier Fishing Lodge: NWT Fishing Smorg *by Duane S. Radford*	62
Plummer's Arctic Lodges: Great Slave Lake *by Duane S. Radford*	68
Taste of Arctic Pike Fishing: Trout Rock Lodge, Northwest Territories *by Duane S. Radford*	75
The Buzz About Mosquito Lake *by Tom Adamchick*	80

5. NUNAVUT

   A River Charmed: Nunavut's Tree River *by Duane S. Radford*   89
   B & J Fly Fishing Adventures, Ekaluk River Char
      by Duane S. Radford   98
   Nueltin Journal *by C. Perry Munro*   103
   The True Gems of the Coppermine River *by Faruk Ekich*   108

6. ONTARIO

   Is the Sutton River the World's Best Brook Trout River?
      by Ken Bailey   117

7. QUEBEC & LABRADOR

   Confessions of a George River (Quebec) Junkie *by Ken Bailey*   127
   Flowers River Lodge (Labrador) *by C. Perry Munro*   139
   Payne River (Quebec) Char *by Mark Anderson*   145

8. YUKON

   Yukon Fishing *by Duane S. Radford*   153
   An Embarrassment of Fishes *by Patrick Walsh*   161
   Operation S.N.A.F.U. *by Jeff Dewsbury*   173
   Grizzly Creek Lodge, Yukon *by Duane S. Radford*   180
   The Last Frontier: Tincup Wilderness Lodge, Yukon
      by Duane S. Radford   186
   Wellesley Lake: Lake Trout Flies & Fly-Fishing Techniques
      by Duane S. Radford   192
   Yukon's Top Stream for 'Bows, the Kathleen River
      by Duane S. Radford   199
   Yukon's Unique Fishing Lodge—Dalton Trail Lodge
      by Duane S. Radford   205

9. A WOMAN'S PERSPECTIVE OF NORTH OF SIXTY
   by Adrienne E. Radford   209

10. SUMMARY *by Duane S. Radford*   223

Remembering Ross Shickler   229
Notes on Sources   233

There will be days when the fishing is better than one's most optimistic forecast, others when it is far worse. Either is a gain over just staying home.

—RODERICK HAIG-BROWN, *Fisherman's Spring,* 1951

INTRODUCTION
by Duane S. Radford

Although I never actually met Ross H. Shickler, I shared a kindred spirit with him as a fellow adventurer. We used to spend hours on the phone talking about fishing—he had a bad case of the northern Canada travel bug. We'd each fished some of the same remote spots, such as Great Bear Lake in the Northwest Territories (NWT) and the famed Tree River in Nunavut, so we had some things in common. We'd experienced the raw beauty of northern Canada and the great fishing opportunities in Canada's North Country. Ross was primarily a spin fisherman, while I'm a keen fly fisher. We shared a passion for fishing in the wilds of northern Canada, particularly for huge lake trout, which Ross considered "North America's greatest game fish"—and rightly so. Ross was so enthralled with lake trout that he and co-author Edward M. Eveland (a fellow educator) wrote a book called *Lake Trout: North America's Greatest Game Fish*, which was published by The Derrydale Press in 2001.

As an aside, Ross and I almost met (fortuitously) in August 2008 at Plummer's Arctic Lodge's Tree River Lodge in Nunavut. He departed on the day I arrived, and sadly, we didn't get to meet in person. I was on the second bush plane coming into the outpost on the Tree River; he left on the first plane that departed before my plane landed. That's fate, I guess, but perhaps something of his spirit was still in camp, and that's how we eventually came together in 2010.

When Ross approached me in 2010 to help him research a book about fishing in northern Canada, a bond was forged that remained strong until his passing. Ross had fished many lakes and streams in Canada: the Coppermine River, lakes and rivers on Victoria Island in the Canadian archipelago, Great Bear Lake (six times), Nueltin Lake, and the Tree River (three times), and he was a seasoned North Country angler.

Due to failing health, Ross was not able to write all the content he had in mind, so he asked me to help him research key topics and search out good stories about fishing in northern Canada by various authors. The research would form the framework for the book, while the articles about various lakes and rivers would serve to illustrate what an itinerant angler could look forward to North of Sixty. Some of America's and Canada's top outdoor writers were approached for articles, and as the book took shape, Ross realized that it should include content beyond fishing for only lake trout, grayling, and Arctic char; it should also extend beyond the territories of the NWT, Nunavut, and Yukon to include northern Quebec and Labrador, and even northern Ontario.

After Ross passed away, his wife Merrie Lyn asked me to co-edit Ross's book to see his dream come true. I hope we've done him proud.

Dedication

LLOYD BULL, world-record holder for lake trout and a veritable institution at Plummer's Arctic Lodge on Great Bear Lake in the NWT. Incredible as it sounds, Lloyd Bull fished Great Bear Lake at least 40 consecutive summers and generously shared his enthusiasm and expertise with fellow anglers throughout his lifetime.

Customized lake trout lure featuring Lloyd Bull's prowess, created by Mark "Doc" Hatton, who presented to Lloyd Bull (and all fishing guests present) at Neiland Bay, Great Bear Lake, NWT, August 2006. (photo credit Mike Shickler)

• • •

HOWARD SHICKLER, Ross's dad, who started it all when he took his little son fishing in Canada.

• • •

ROSS H. SHICKLER, whose wife Merrie Lyn wished to dedicate this book to the memory of her late husband. Ross dreamed of publishing a book about fishing in northern Canada—in particular, the region popularly known as the area North of Sixty and fondly referred to as the North Country.

Although Ross passed away at the age of 77 before he was able to achieve this goal, Merrie Lyn and co-editor Duane S. Radford have striven to honour his vision by publishing this book posthumously. Ross began fishing at the age of three and enjoyed a lifelong passion for the sport; in fact, his business card and website both cited "Angler and Author" beneath his name as a testament to his zeal. The back of Ross's business card even featured the following striking photo taken by Doug Geertgens with the caption: *A fiery Arctic sunset greets late-evening anglers— Great Bear Lake, Northwest Territories, Canada.*

Ross, you are deeply missed.

CHAPTER 1

HOMAGE:
A TRIBUTE TO LLOYD BULL
by **Mark Anderson**

> The late MARK ANDERSON was a field editor for Canada's largest outdoor magazine, *Outdoor Canada*, and was a well-known Canadian writer who wrote this Homage in the May 2012 issue of *Outdoor Canada*. "First Lloyd, now Ross: it's sad to lose such great men and passionate anglers," Mark Anderson lamented in an e-mail to Duane S. Radford. Ross H. Shickler met Lloyd Bull at Plummer's Arctic Lodges on Great Bear Lake, the flagship of Plummer's iconic chain of outstanding fishing lodges in the NWT and Nunavut. Ross interviewed Lloyd by phone and through correspondence for his book *Lake Trout: North America's Greatest Game Fish* (2001), and later travelled to Lloyd's home in the state of New York after Lloyd retired. Ross very much admired Lloyd, and he was emphatic that this tribute to him be featured prominently in this book.

Lloyd Bull and his wife (L) Arlene Grashoff Bull.
(Photo credit Mark "Doc" Hatton)

Lloyd Bull

Farewell to Great Bear Lake's Legendary Laker Taker

I'm in a cabin on a trout lake in Quebec and Lloyd Bull is telling me a story. About the time he meticulously engineered a hunt so as to drive a nice buck directly into the crosshairs of a perfectly situated shooter, the greenhorn at the trigger fell asleep. "I kept waiting for the shot," said the legendary outdoorsman, voice rising with incredulity and wonder. "No shot!"

Two years later I still smile at the memory. Whether hunting or fishing, Laker Lloyd Bull always took his shot. And some of those shots took place in Canada's Far North, which the Adirondack, NY-born adventurer considered his spiritual second home. He explored the North extensively, eventually focusing his attention on Great Bear Lake, mapping the shoals by hand and pioneering the art of hooking and landing monster lake trout (hint: big spoons, loose drags—"Ya gotta let 'em run."). His prowess eventually resulted in two IGFA lake trout world records, including a 72-pound goliath he battled to the boat in 1995—a record that stands to this day.

His biggest contribution to northern angling, however, took place after his boat capsized and his native guide perished in the icy chop. Lloyd responded by helping craft a list of recommendations and protocols for enhancing safety on the notoriously dangerous lake, including better boats and survival equipment, improved training of guides, and a "buddy system" where boats always travel in pairs.

In the end, skin cancer got him, and he died in January 2012 at the age of 86. The disease was almost certainly caused by a life spent hunting and fishing in the sun, but I don't think Lloyd would have had it any other way. Indeed, as recently as a week before his death, too weak to stand, he was still asking his son to take him out fishing. That was Lloyd Bull. He took his shot.

As a further tribute to Lloyd Bull, the following letter from Plummer's Arctic Lodges staff was sent to Lloyd and his family on December 20, 2011, shortly before he passed.

Dear Lloyd and family,

We here at Plummer's Lodges just wanted to wish everyone a Merry Christmas from your Canadian friends and hope that you all enjoy the holiday season.

We missed Lloyd the last couple of years and were deeply saddened when he told us he would not be back for another visit. Neiland Bay is a quieter place now without Lloyd and his stories, though his stories will continue to be told. Lloyd taught a lot about fishing to many people up at Great Bear, and many of his lessons continue to be executed on the water every summer. Lloyd may have caught more giant lake trout than anyone on the planet, and obviously his world record fish that hangs proudly above the bar at the main lodge will continue to be a source of inspiration and motivation for anglers for years to come. No one visits Great Bear without staring at that fish, mouth slightly agape, suddenly aware that they too are fishing in the land of giants. Perhaps the only ones who are not saddened by Lloyd's retirement from Great Bear would be the lake trout themselves, for they are likely relieved that arguably the most successful hog-hunter of all time is not going to fool them again with a sharp shiny spoon.

Take care Lloyd and enjoy time with your family. You will be missed up at Great Bear but you will not be forgotten.

Sincerely,

Your Plummer's Lodges Friends

CHAPTER 2

NORTH OF SIXTY

by **Duane S. Radford and Ross H. Shickler**

North of Sixty covers the area in northern Canada north of the 60th parallel that separates the country's remote northern territories—NWT, Nunavut, and Yukon from the southern Canadian provinces of British Columbia, Alberta, Saskatchewan, and Manitoba, and also refers to the area north of this parallel in Quebec and Labrador in eastern Canada. It should be noted that most Canadians normally refer to the Northwest Territories as simply the NWT. These territories are very sparsely populated and loaded with thousands of lakes and streams, many of which feature outstanding fishing for lake trout, grayling, Arctic char, and brook trout in eastern Canada, as well as Atlantic salmon in Quebec and Labrador.

GEOGRAPHY

Map of Canada: the 60th parallel separates the southern provinces of British Columbia, Alberta, Saskatchewan, and Manitoba from the northern territories of Yukon, Northwest Territories (NWT), and Nunavut.

The co-editors had many discussions about the title of this book; Ross's original suggestion was that it be called *Fishing Northern Canada for Lake Trout, Grayling, and Arctic Char*, while Duane thought it should perhaps be called *Fishing North of Sixty*. After Ross passed away, Duane decided to go with Ross's original title as that's what this book is primarily about—fishing for lake trout, which Ross considered "North America's greatest game fish"—but also Arctic grayling and Arctic char. As the various chapters were scoped out, it was eventually decided that while the focus of the book would remain on the area called North of Sixty primarily in the NWT, Nunavut, and Yukon, content would also be added for northern Quebec and Labrador (formerly known as the Ungava), and in special cases for northern Ontario.

There is a clear constitutional distinction between Canadian *provinces* and *territories*. While the provinces exercise constitutional powers in their own right, the territories exercise delegated powers under the authority of the Parliament of Canada. Historically, this authority has meant that the northern territories were largely governed by federal officials out of Canada's capital city of Ottawa, Ontario; however, over the past 40 years, major changes have occurred in the governance of these territories. For example, federal statutes have established a legislative assembly and executive council for each territory, and province-like powers are increasingly being transferred or "devolved" to territorial governments by the Government of Canada. This process, known as *devolution*, provides greater local decision-making and accountability.

In addition to Canada's northern territories, in the far eastern region of Canada, parts of Labrador and Quebec also lie north of the 60th parallel. Newfoundland and Labrador are collectively one province, as Quebec is a distinct province, and the broad area of northern Quebec and Labrador was once officially called the Ungava. The district of Ungava was a regional administrative district of Canada's former Northwest Territories from 1895 to 1920, then it effectively ceased operation in 1912. It covered the northern portion of what is today Quebec, the interior of Labrador, and the offshore islands to the west and north of Quebec, which are now part of Nunavut. The name Ungava is of Inuktitut origin, meaning "towards the open water." This term is believed to be in reference to the lands inhabited by the Ungava Inuit, who lived at the mouth of the Arnaud River, which flows into Ungava Bay in northern Quebec.

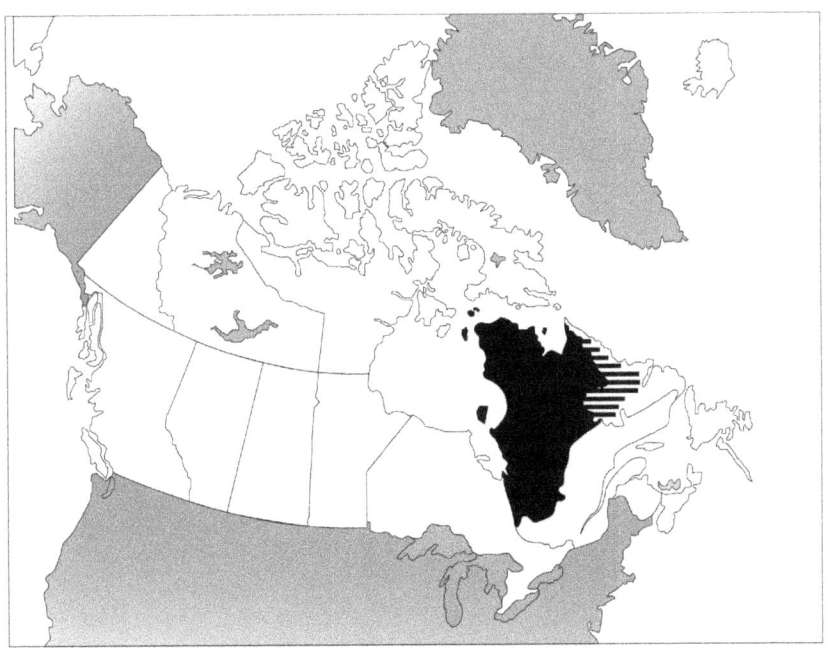

District of Ungava at its creation in 1895, superimposed over a modern-day map of Canada.

> The overall area (in square kilometres) of the NWT (1,183,085), Nunavut (1,936,113), and the Yukon (474,391) is huge: 3,593,589. By comparison, the area of Texas is 696,200 square kilometres, or 19% of the size of these large territories.

The capital cities of each territory are Iqaluit (Nunavut), Yellowknife (NWT), and Whitehorse (Yukon). Note that there is no "u" following the "q" in Iqaluit as the word "Iqualuit" has an altogether different, unpleasant meaning in the Inuit vocabulary. The territories are sparsely populated (based on the latest 2011 census)—Nunavut (31,906), NWT (41,462), and Yukon (33,897) —yet encompass a huge area, some 39.3 percent of Canada. The following table (area in square kilometres) illustrates their relative size and the amount of fresh water in each territory as compared with the rest of Canada.

Territory	Land Area	Freshwater Area	Area in % of Whole Canada
NWT	1,183,085	163,021	13.5%
Nunavut	1,936,113	157,079	21.0%
Yukon	474,391	8,052	4.8%

> It should be noted that, officially, measurements are in metric in Canada, not imperial units (i.e., distances are in km not miles; weights are in kg not pounds; temperatures are in degrees Celsius not Fahrenheit). Another anomaly is the way Canadians spell "licence" instead of "license," which follows British conventions. This also applies to words such as harbour, humour, honour, etc. that contain a "u." Generally, the Canadian vocabulary is used throughout this book, although equivalencies for km and miles are noted. Because anglers normally use the English units of pounds, inches, and feet when they're sizing their catch, generally no metric equivalents will be cited in this book when referring to the size of fish.

This area boasts a great deal of fresh water for fishing, roughly comparable to the amount in both Ontario (158,654 sq. km) and Quebec (176,928 sq. km), two eastern Canadian provinces combined for the NWT and Nunavut; and much more than in Alberta (19,531 sq. km) and British Columbia (19,549 sq. km), considered by many to be western Canadian fishing hotspots for trout and char.

The very name "territories" has a certain romance to it: the NWT, Nunavut, and Yukon are truly Canada's last frontiers, complete with some of the best fishing and unspoiled landscapes in the whole country. Nunavut was created in 1999 by splitting off the eastern Arctic area from the NWT, which was earlier inhabited primarily by people of Inuit ancestry. (Inuit has replaced the word "Eskimo"—which means "the people"—in the Canadian vocabulary. Aboriginals in Canada and Greenland generally view the name Eskimo as pejorative, and it is not considered polite to use this term nowadays. Inuit is a collective noun with the singular being "Inuk.") Majestic mountains, vast boreal forests, lakes as large as inland seas, mighty rivers, and the seemingly endless barren grounds in the far north—beyond the very reaches of civilization—typify the region North of Sixty in northern Canada.

ANGLING REGULATIONS

> Anglers will be very pleased to know that angling licences are inexpensive and regulations are relatively simple throughout Canada's northern territories, Quebec, and Labrador.

With the relative simplicity of sport fishing regulations in the NWT, Nunavut, and Yukon—compared with what are generally long, detailed, (and often) complex regulations in the various Canadian provinces and National Parks, including Newfoundland, Labrador, and Quebec, which are referred to specifically in the following section of this chapter—the regulations, per se, are only a few pages long for the most part. Although more lengthy in the Yukon, the majority are fairly straightforward, with most of the regulation text being of the information and education category—especially with regard to boating safety and being aware of bears, in particular.

Seasonal fishing licences are relatively inexpensive, especially for non-residents, as per the following breakdown, and haven't changed over the past several years:

Jurisdiction	Resident	Resident Canadian	Non-Resident
Newfoundland and Labrador	$17	$53 (salmon) $8 (trout)	$53 (salmon) $8 (trout)
NWT	$10	$20	$40
Nunavut	$10	$20	$40
Quebec (except Atlantic salmon)	$20.41 (under 65) $16.18 (over 65)	$65.77	$65.77
Yukon	$15	$25	$35

It's also possible to get 3-day licences in the NWT and Nunavut at the following costs:

3-Day Licence	Resident Canadian	Non-Resident
NWT	$15	$30
Nunavut	$15	$30

In the Yukon, 6-day and 1-day licences are available at the following rates:

Licence Fees	6 days	1 day
Canadian Resident	$15	$10
Non-Resident	$20	$10

In Quebec, they offer 7-day, 3-day, and 1-day licences (general and for Atlantic salmon); note that the 7- and 1-day permits are for non-residents only. Sport fishing licences (except for Atlantic salmon) are shown in the following table for Quebec:

Licence Fees	7 days	3 days	1 day
Residents	n/a	$11.68	n/a
Non-Residents	$44.02	$28.64	$12.99

In the NWT, there are additional First Nation's "Validations" that apply to the Great Bear Lake Special Management Area, Inuvialuit Settlement Region, Gwich'in Settlement Area, and Sahtu Settlement Area. Likewise, in the Yukon, (free) special permits are required to fish in Tatimain Lake or Wellesley Lake.

In Newfoundland and Labrador, non-resident anglers must be guided. The regulations state that north of 52°N in Labrador, a non-resident shall not angle inland waters without engaging the services of an outfitter, with some exceptions specified in the angling regulations. A licenced guide is guilty of an offence if as a guide, he/she accompanies at the same time more than two non-residents licenced to fish.

In Quebec non-residents who wish to fish north of the 52nd parallel (Zones 19 south, 22 north, 23, 24, and 29), or east of the rivière Saint-Augustin (Zone 19 south), must use the services of an outfitter.

Fishing regulations are relatively simple in each jurisdiction and can be obtained online at the following websites (which are current at the time of publication, but updated site addresses may be given at the beginning of a new year, depending on the territory):

NEWFOUNDLAND AND LABRADOR
http://bit.ly/newfoundland-and-labrador

NWT
http://bit.ly/fishing-reg-2014-2015-NWT

NUNAVUT
http://bit.ly/fishing-guide-nunavut

QUEBEC
http://bit.ly/fishing-guide-quebec

YUKON
http://bit.ly/fishing-guide-yukon

In certain areas of Canada's North Country, catch-and-release fishing is a sensitive issue with some members of local First Nations who feel that fish should only be caught for food, not for recreational purposes. For this reason, anglers should keep traditional use of fish in the back of their minds when angling in the North Country, which is still a highly important source of sustenance for many First Nations people. Also, because fish can be easy to catch (at times), it's necessary to practice some self-restraint (and limit your catches) to keep angling mortality to a minimum. Northern waters may have a high-standing crop of fish, but they are generally quite unproductive—it takes many years for the stocks to build up. Fish typically grow slowly and have a very long life span—it's not uncommon for large lake trout to be 30–40+ years of age.

RECREATIONAL FISHING SURVEYS

> Ongoing recreational fishing surveys conducted at five-year intervals by Canada's federal, provincial, and territorial governments since 1975 substantiate that fishing pressure in Canada's North Country remains very light, with uncrowded waters and excellent catch rates to this day.

There is relatively little fishing pressure in the NWT, Nunavut, and Yukon, based on information obtained from the *2010 Recreational Fishing Survey of Canada* report, the last year for which data are available, and earlier similar reports. In Canada the federal, provincial, and territorial governments jointly survey recreational fishing every five years and have been doing so since 1975. The following information provides a snapshot of the most recent recreational fishing survey data for these territories. Comparable data cannot be presented for the provinces of Newfoundland and Labrador or Quebec because most of their lands lie south of the 60th parallel, and the data set is tabulated at a provincial, not regional, level.

Territory	Licenced Anglers	Total (including non-residents)
NWT	5008	10746
Nunavut	659	1410
Yukon	8380	15141
Total	**14,047**	**27,297**

Granted, these territories have a short fishing season, at best from late May/June through the end of September (or thereabouts), but it's still a surprise that fishing pressure is so light, considering it is often impacted by the vagaries of forest fires and inclement weather in this area. For example, a bad fire season in the Yukon and late breakup in the NWT in 2004 scared off some visitors and delayed lodge openings, respectively.

About half of the anglers in Canada's North Country are non-residents. "Fishing tourism" is obviously huge in this area, where it's a dream for many anglers to go on a fishing trip, and it's made easier nowadays with more and better air and road connections. In a cost analysis with similar adventure packages—whether at Caribbean or Rocky Mountain resorts, or on luxury cruises—the prices are comparable. Canada's North Country is still a paradise on earth for fishermen, offering excellent fishing on uncrowded lakes and streams with lots of big fish, unspoiled landscapes, and wildlife aplenty.

GEARING UP FOR A NORTH OF SIXTY FISHING TRIP

> There are no corner stores, so to speak, or handy tackle shops once you leave the capital cities in the Yukon (Whitehorse), NWT (Yellowknife), and Nunavut (Iqaluit), so sage anglers will ensure they have everything they might need for their northern fishing adventure before they board a plane for their final destination.

Because first-time visitors often do not have a good appreciation for just how cold it can be in Canada's North Country—sometimes even in the middle of summer—it's a good idea to ask the lodge owner for a checklist of what to bring. Many of the lakes are huge and it's impossible to see from one shore to the other; on some of the huge lakes, such as Great Bear Lake and Great Slave Lake, the summer water temperature may not go above 10°C. Also, it's not unusual to travel for an hour between fishing spots, so wind chill can be a real issue. Ensuring you have the proper clothing will therefore be essential, so although there will likely be weight restrictions on your luggage, don't skimp on quality gear, which will make your trip that much more enjoyable.

It's always best to prepare for extreme weather as you may run into rain, or even snowstorms, during the summer, while other times it may be hotter than a pistol. No matter the season, however, rain gear is essential, and you'll want to dress in layers with waterproof outer clothing that will break the wind. This is especially important if you're on a boat on cold water during a long haul. I also recommend packing some lightweight, polyester thermal underwear that dries twice as fast as cotton, just in case you run into a cold spell or need it when boating or wading in often ice-cold northern waters.

For footwear, pack gum boots for camp and field activities, as well as chest waders with felt-lined wading boots if you intend to fish offshore or in streams; duck boots and rubber sandals or running shoes will be good choices for camp life, depending on the weather.

Protecting your hands and eyes will be vital, so you'll want to pack wool gloves (both with full and half fingers), a toque, and a long-brimmed baseball hat—preferably light in colour so as not to absorb a lot of summer sun—to wear when fishing to shade your eyes. Polarized sunglasses are also essential when on the water to protect your eyes against harmful ultra-violet rays, and as an aid in being able to see the lake and stream bottom. And don't forget the sunscreen and lip balm—the days are often long in the North Country!

There are many brands of outdoor clothing for fishing enthusiasts, with some of the top lines being Columbia Sportswear Company, Orvis, and Simms. For maximum protection from biting insects, "The Original Bug Shirt" is recommended for those averse to black flies and mosquitoes (call 1-800-998-9096 or visit www.bugshirt.com to place an order, or obtain from Mountain Equipment Co-op stores in Canada). Mosquitoes are generally worse early in the summer and black flies, closer to autumn. No matter what, however, you should bring facial protection from biting insects, as well as insect repellent with DEET.

When you pack, place your fishing gear and clothes in soft, waterproof duffel bags that can be fitted into a floatplane or helicopter, with hard cases for fishing rods. Eddie Bauer and Mountain Equipment Co-op (in Canada) carry a good line of both small and extra-large duffel bags for your gear, and rod cases are available at many sporting goods stores. Greenheart dual rod carrying cases can be fitted with reels and taken along in boats once you hit fish camp, and protective covers for your reels are a good idea if you'll be fishing from outboard boats. Don't forget to pack some duct tape to tape rod cases together, if necessary.

Anglers must also be ever-cognizant of bears North of Sixty, which are not uncommon and can be very dangerous, especially barren-ground grizzlies, polar bears, and black bears. Bring some pepper spray and familiarize yourself with how to use it before your trip. Also, pack a flare gun with a supply of bear bangers and test it before you leave home to ensure it works and that you're familiar with how to fire it, if necessary. Bear bangers may be either centre or rim fire, and a flare gun must be calibrated to fire properly. Some flare guns have interchangeable firing pins that can be set to launch either centre or rim fire, whereas others will only fire one way, but not both. To be safe, load a bear banger in your flare gun when out fishing and keep it in an easily accessible place.

Though one hopes to never need it, you'll want to make sure you're covered for an air ambulance by your local health plan in case of an emergency before you venture north, or that you purchase insurance with an agency such as MedjetAssist (http://medjetassist.com or call 800-5ASSIST), which provides coverage for not only the United States, but also Canada.

Because it's not uncommon for planes to be grounded because of bad weather, you will also need to be prepared to stay in the bush, if necessary. Having an emergency survival gear kit on your person at all times is vital, both for air travel into remote areas and when on the ground or water. It's also crucial to wear non-flammable clothing when travelling by air. If a plane does go down or you get swamped and have to make for shore, a safety whistle should also be part of your gear.

When it comes to equipment, a #4–6-weight rod will be adequate for fly fishers for Arctic grayling, but for the larger species such as Arctic char, Inconnu, lake trout, and northern pike, a #8–9 weight rod is a must, with up to a #10-weight for pike. Floating line, sink tip, and full sink are standard for the variety of conditions you're likely to encounter, with at least 100 yards of backing. Take a selection of dry flies for Arctic grayling and a range of streamers for other species.

Your tackle box must have a good supply of lures, spare rod tips, fishing line, etc., and you should definitely bring an extra rod (or two), as it's not unusual to break rods when trying to land big fish in Canada's far north. Gear up for big, feisty fish with sturdy rods and reels capable of handling fish anywhere from 10–50 pounds, at least. Line weights, swivels, and leaders must all be capable of bearing such weights; large northern pike can destroy the gears in even the highest quality spinning reels. Bear in mind that the world's largest lake trout was taken in 1961 in the Saskatchewan portion of Lake Athabasca—which straddles the Alberta/Saskatchewan border just south of the 60th parallel—and weighed 46.3 kg (101.9 pounds), so folks aren't exaggerating when they say there are big fish in Canada's North County.

Pike enthusiasts will want to pack needle-nose pliers with wire cutters (or long-handled hook disgorgers) and soft-tipped jaw spreaders (fish gags), as well as titanium, wire, or woven monofilament leaders and rubber (claw or grip) handling gloves.

Check to see if the lodge has fish cradles to handle large pike and lake trout, which are essential for photo ops.

In addition to the gear already mentioned, it goes without saying that you should always pack a Leatherman full-size multi-tool (or equivalent) to make repairs to your equipment, if necessary. A hook sharpener is also essential to keep hook tips honed—especially when fishing barbless hooks—to get more consistent catches and to minimize hook throws on large, tough-jawed northern fish. A dry pack and a waterproof day pack to store extra gear is also a great idea for trips where you'll be on the water during the day.

To round off your checklist, make sure to pack the usual toiletries, first-aid kit contents, fly vest and day pack, flashlight, camera and soft carrying case (with film or memory cards and extra batteries), gratuities, and fishing accessories you think you'll need.

Remember: be prepared for contingencies that might arise during your trip. You can usually buy a fishing licence at a fishing lodge, but there won't be a shop around the corner from the lodge or your camp, or a nearby grocery store with liquor on the shelves. If you pack everything you'll need in soft carrying bags, except for rods, which must be in protective cases, you'll be well prepared for your fishing adventure in Canada's northern territories.

FISHING LODGES

> Fishing enthusiasts are encouraged to research government travel websites, travel planners, and brochures, as well as fishing lodge brochures and websites while making plans for a trip North of Sixty, to fully enjoy and appreciate the great fishing opportunities for what might well be a trip of a lifetime.

You don't actually need to stay at a lodge to enjoy fishing in Canada's North Country, but if you haven't ventured to the NWT,

Nunavut, or the Yukon before, it's probably a good way to start—unless you have a local to show you the ropes.

There's nothing quite like a visit to a northern fishing lodge for an unforgettable vacation; and if you go during the summer, the long northern days will energize you and make you feel young again. A word of advice: at first glance, some lodges may seem expensive, but if you break down the costs of food, lodging, boats/gas, and often at least one day of guide services, and compare the overall costs with other vacation packages, you'll be getting a good deal. Bear in mind that virtually everything at a lodge must be flown in, such as fuel and propane, and charter costs are very expensive. Americans should check out the exchange rate relative to the Canadian dollar to capitalize on bargains.

At first glance, the plethora of fishing lodges in the NWT, Nunavut, and Yukon is a bit staggering when considering where to go, what to fish for, costs, and travel arrangements. As such, you'll want to start with a visit to the territorial tourism websites or call centres (as follows), where you can make an online or telephone request for a travel brochure and/or travel planner. Variously called "vacation guides" or "explorers' guide[books]," travel brochure and/or travel planner documents list the various fishing lodges in each territory; they also provide maps, travel planning tips, various adventure packages, and accommodations in the different travel regions in each territory.

NWT
www.explorenwt.com (1-800-661-0788)

NUNAVUT
www.nunavuttourism.com (1-866-NUNAVUT (686-2888))

YUKON
www.touryukon.com (1-800-661-0494)

For those anglers interested in a trip to Newfoundland and Labrador or Quebec, check out the following websites:

NEWFOUNDLAND AND LABRADOR

www.newfoundlandlabrador.com (1-800-563-6353)

QUEBEC

www.bonjourquebec.com (1-877- BONJOUR)

The website images of floatplanes, enormous fish, canoes beside pristine waters, and majestic landscapes will conjure up all sorts of utopian expectations and give you a good outlook of your prospects right from the get-go. Explore the following sites and your journey will begin, if only in your dreams. You can also request brochures (and often CD-ROMs) from particular lodges.

NWT

www.spectacularnwt.com

NEWFOUNDLAND AND LABRADOR

www.newfoundlandlabrador.com

NUNAVUT

www.nunavuttourism.com

QUEBEC

www.fishinginquebec.com

YUKON

www.sportsmansresource.com

Most of the lodges have their own individual websites that illustrate all things important to the travelling fisherman; you may also wish to visit your local sportsmen shows, or speak directly with lodge operators to get a firsthand impression.

There's a variety of sport fish species in the NWT (Arctic char, Arctic grayling, bull trout, burbot, Dolly Varden, Inconnu, lake trout, northern pike, and lake whitefish); Nunavut (Arctic char, Arctic grayling, lake trout, northern pike, walleye, brook trout, and lake whitefish); and Yukon (rainbow trout, lake trout, Dolly Varden, bull trout, Arctic char, Arctic grayling, northern pike, burbot, broad whitefish, lake whitefish, and Inconnu, as well as several species of salmon, seasonally: Chinook, coho, chum, sockeye, and kokanee). In Newfoundland and Labrador and in Quebec, both Atlantic salmon and eastern brook trout are keystone sport-fishing attractions, and these provinces are renowned for excellent fishing for these species, as well as Arctic char, lake trout, and northern pike.

Most fishing lodges in Canada's northern territories offer package deals and will provide all meals and accommodations, often including a shore lunch or two, as well as bar service. Some lodges even have lounges; others use a cash bar or honour system. Many have all the amenities of home, such as flush toilets, hot and cold running water, and showers. Most are fly-in lodges, but some can be reached by vehicle.

There are 63 fishing lodges in the NWT and seven each in Nunavut and Yukon. There are, however, other lodges that provide guided fishing trips, although their primary orientation isn't for fishing.

> A sampling of articles written by some of the best outdoor writers in Canada and the United States—based on both do-it-yourself fishing trips, as well as trips at several key lodges and on various lakes and rivers in each of the territories—is provided in this book to give the reader an idea of what to expect during a fishing trip in northern Canada. This includes northern Quebec and Labrador, as well as northern Ontario, famed for its world-class brook trout fishing and the Coronation Gulf near Kugluktuk.

Let's imagine that you've made plans to visit a fishing lodge—or intend to go it alone on a fishing trip—in Canada's North Country. How are you going to get there? Do you plan to drive or fly? What should you bring in the way of fishing gear, etc.? And, what should you expect once you arrive at a fishing lodge, if that's your destination?

If you're searching for ways to travel by air to the NWT, Nunavut, or the Yukon, and how to get around once you arrive, check out the following websites for further details:

NWT

www.nwt.worldweb.com/Transportation/Airlines/

NEWFOUNDLAND & LABRADOR

www.newfoundlandlabrador.com/planyourtrip/gettinghere

NUNAVUT

www.nunavut.worldweb.com/Transportation/Airlines/

QUEBEC

www.skyscanner.ca/flights-to/yqb/airlines-that-fly-to-quebec-airport.html

YUKON

www.yukon.worldweb.com/Transportation/Airlines/

If you wish to drive, you can take the Mackenzie Highway from Edmonton to Yellowknife in the NWT (1,508 km), or the Alaska Highway from Edmonton to Whitehorse in the Yukon (2,070 km)—both are paved roads.

Regarding lodge selection, consider the following options:

- ❖ Approach lodge owners directly at sportsmen shows for face-to-face discussions.
- ❖ Check out lodge websites and request a brochure and CD, if available, to learn about fishing opportunities and lodge attractions.
- ❖ Talk to the lodge owners and their fishing guides over the phone.

❖ Check out references and inquire about lodge facilities, meals and accommodations, boats and motors, and the daily routine, such as how you'll actually get to the lodge, services if you must travel by air (e.g., do they provide a shuttle service from the airport/local motel or hotel, or to the floatplane departure dock?); when fishing is generally hot; and how many guests stay at the lodge per week.

Most lodges will supply you with a checklist of items you should bring to make the most of your vacation. It's absolutely essential that you bring all the items on the list and stay within the weight restrictions listed for flights into lodges. These checklists are also useful guides if you're going it alone.

Some lodges provide fully-guided trips while others provide guide services for orientation purposes only, charging for extra guided days, after which you'll be on your own. Prepare for the unexpected—it's not unusual to have to change plans because of poor weather, so you must be able to modify your plans as the need arises. For example, it may be too rough to fish a lake and you'll have to switch to a river or stream—or even stay in camp if the weather is severe. With a bit of planning and organization and some cooperation from the weatherman, you should be in for the trip of a lifetime on your fishing trip to Canada's North Country.

FISH ID & BIOLOGY 101

It's sad to say but there's not a lot of widely available popular literature regarding fish biology, distribution, and identification for the most common game fish of northern Canada, so a brief synopsis is in order for Arctic char, Arctic grayling, Atlantic salmon, eastern brook trout, lake trout, and northern pike. Scientific textbooks, such as Scott and Crossman's treatise *Freshwater Fishes of Canada* (1973) and the *Freshwater Fishes of Northwestern Canada and Alaska* by J. D. McPhail and C. C. Lindsey

(1973) provide the most definitive information, but here is an introduction to each to give you a nice overview.

 Arctic Char

SCIENTIFIC NAME: *Salvelinus alpinus* (*Salvelinus*: an old name of the char (charr) family; *alpinus*: of the mountains)

BIOLOGY: There may be both anadromous (migrating up rivers from the sea to spawn) and landlocked populations. Arctic char are carnivorous; adults feed mainly on small fish and aquatic invertebrates. Their growth rate is slow; for example, in Canada's eastern Arctic it takes 10–15 years for anadromous char to reach five pounds in weight. Age of maturity varies across their range from about 7–12 years of age. The oldest char recorded from the North American Arctic were at least 24 years old. Spawning occurs in the autumn over gravel beds, in lakes, and in pools below rapids in rivers, according to McPhail and Lindsey (1970). The burst speed of a fresh Arctic char is second to none among freshwater fish. They are famed for their table fare and are on the menu of fine dining rooms across Canada and in some parts of the United States.

DISTRIBUTION: Arctic char are native to northern parts of the northern hemisphere, and in Canada occur in some coastal areas and islands in the Canadian Arctic Archipelago and the Ungava area with migrations in rivers to spawn.

IDENTIFICATION: Round large spots (often a violet-pink colour) on the back and sides of a silver body (fresh fish from the ocean).

CHAPTER 2 | NORTH *of* SIXTY

Arctic Grayling

SCIENTIFIC NAME: *Thymallus arcticus* (*Thymallus*: an ancient name of the grayling, pertaining to the fish's odor of thyme, which may or may not always be noticeable; *arcticus*: of the Arctic)

BIOLOGY: Typically, grayling are found only in cool, unpolluted streams and lakes as they're very sensitive to poor water quality and intolerant of polluted waters. While they feed mainly on aquatic invertebrates, they will occasionally eat small fish and terrestrial insects. Spawning occurs in the spring in streams, when males defend their spawning territories, and the eggs are buried in the gravel. Their maximum age is in the range of 11–12 years according to Scott and Crossman (1973); the maximum size can exceed 2 kg (5 pounds) in Canada's North Country. With regard to the smell of thyme, it can be very noticeable on some fish, but not at all on others.

DISTRIBUTION: The range of Arctic grayling goes across northern Canada in the Yukon, NWT, and western Nunavut (as well as northern British Columbia, Alberta, Saskatchewan, and Manitoba), but not on islands in the Canadian Archipelago or Ungava.

IDENTIFICATION: Usually a strikingly coloured fish with a dark purple dorsal surface, or blue-black to blue-grey, with grey or dark blue sides and a pinkish iridescence with a large, prominent dorsal fin, particularly in males.

 *Atlantic Salmon*

SCIENTIFIC NAME: *Salmo salar* (*Salmo*: from the Latin word meaning salmon; *salar*: old name from "salio" meaning to leap)

BIOLOGY: According to Scott and Crossman (1973), the Atlantic salmon is the classic anadromous fish, which spawn in freshwater streams. The adults return to sea and the young remain in fresh water for 2–3 years, at which time they move downstream to the sea for one or more years, feeding and growing before returning to fresh water to spawn. Spawning occurs in October and November in Canada. Females select a gravel-bottom riffle area above or below a pool to excavate a redd, where her fertilized eggs are deposited and covered with gravel. Anadromous salmon may weight up to about 36 kg (80 pounds); adults don't die after spawning and may spawn more than once. There's nothing quite as unnerving as to be casting in a pool during the autumn as dozens of salmon leap skyward and splash back into the pool. They can be notoriously difficult to catch.

DISTRIBUTION: Eastern Canada and northeastern United States along the North Atlantic Ocean, from the Ungava region of northern Quebec south to the Connecticut River in New England.

IDENTIFICATION: In the sea, silvery on sides and white below, with the back brown, green, or blue. On entering fresh water, adults lose their silvery colour and become darker, taking on a bronze and dark brown colouration, sometimes with reddish spots on their heads and bodies.

Eastern Brook Trout

SCIENTIFIC NAME: *Salvelinus fontinalis* (*Salvelinus*: an old name of the char (charr) family; *fontinalis*: living in springs)

BIOLOGY: Brook trout (also known as Eastern brook trout or speckled trout) are members of the char family, found in both lakes and streams. They spawn in the autumn or late summer, usually in streams where females dig a redd in the gravel and lay their eggs, but they can also spawn in lakes where there are areas of upwelling on gravel beds. They can reach a large size, but tend to stunt when overpopulated in both lakes and streams. According to Scott and Crossman (1973), the maximum size for brook trout was a 6.6-kg (14.5-pound) fish caught in Rabbit Rapids, Nipigon River, Ontario, in 1915, although there have been unofficial reports of larger fish from Labrador.

DISTRIBUTION: Primarily in eastern Canada and the northeastern United States; however, they have been widely stocked across both countries.

IDENTIFICATION: Brook trout have black markings on their dorsal fin, red spots with blue halos, and a square tail (not deeply forked) with a deep body. They tend to be green with vermiculations (i.e., marbling; wavy or wormlike lines) on the back, with white leading edges on their fins.

 *Lake Trout*

SCIENTIFIC NAME: *Salvelinus namaycush* (*Salvelinus*: an old name of the char (charr); *namaycush*: an Indian name, meaning "dweller of the deep")

BIOLOGY: Lake trout are members of the char family that spawn in the autumn. Females broadcast their eggs over rubble and cobble on windswept shallow shoals and are largely bottom feeders with tremendous olfactory powers. They are predacious, largely piscivorous (feeding on other fish), grow slowly, mature late, and tend to live a long life (up to 25+ years). Noted Canadian ichthyologists have said that lake trout are just waiting for the next ice age to break out. Why? They're creatures of cold, deep, unproductive lakes and streams in northern Canada and thrive in these harsh environments. The maximum size can reach at least 122 cm (48 inches) with a weight of 46.4 kg (102 pounds), according to McPhail and Lindsey (1970), but they are usually much smaller.

DISTRIBUTION: According to Scott and Crossman (1973), lake trout naturally occur only in North America, and their range coincides most closely with the limits of the Pleistocene glaciation.

IDENTIFICATION: Lake trout have pale spots on their dorsal fins and deeply forked tails. Their body colouration is typically either silver or brown, but in some lakes, can be ink black. They have white leading edges on their fins.

 *Northern Pike*

SCIENTIFIC NAME: *Esox lucius* (*Esox*: a kind of pike; *lucius*: the Latin name for the pike)

BIOLOGY: Northern pike are found both in lakes and slow-moving streams and rivers; they prefer relatively shallow, weedy, clear waters along the shoreline, and they tend to be ambush predators, feeding on fish as adults. They spawn in the spring, often in shallow marshes connected to lakes or flooded vegetation in shallow bays, where the adhesive eggs are broadcast and stick to vegetation. There's a common myth that pike lose their teeth, which is not true. The maximum length is about 133 cm (4 feet) with a weight of about 25+ kg (55 pounds). Pike fillets cooked as a shore lunch are highly rated by gourmets.

DISTRIBUTION: Northern pike are widely distributed all across the Yukon, NWT, western Nunavut, and northern Quebec and Labrador.

IDENTIFICATION: Adults are typically olive or brownish-green dorsally, with large irregular white or greenish spots laterally in oblique rows, with moderately forked tails and toothy mouths.

CLIMATE CHANGE

Greenhouse gases are contributing to global warming, which is causing climate change, an issue of serious concern in Canada's North Country because the plants and animals are adapted to a cold subarctic and arctic climate. In the north there are already reports that the weather is more unpredictable and doesn't follow the patterns it did historically.

The weather also apparently changes faster than it used to, with storms blowing up unexpectedly. There are even reports that both the length and timing of seasons have changed; weather monitoring in Nunavut indicates that the period from 2000–2010 was the warmest decade in modern times. Global warming in the NWT, Nunavut, and the Yukon will have serious consequences if not addressed, as the temperature in these territories is warming faster than in the rest of Canada. Also, the Arctic has warmed at a higher rate than the annual global average temperature. The upshot of global warming on the loss of sea ice and its impact on polar bears has received the most publicity, but there will be many other serious environmental consequences. It's not possible to detail the potential impacts on wildlife and Arctic vegetation in this book, but we will review some of the implications of climate change arising from global warming on fish.

The changes in weather caused by global warming may result in either early or late breakup on lakes and rivers in this area. Late breakup can result in a loss in productivity in both lakes and streams, which can translate into fewer and smaller fish in the longer term. Cooling in the autumn may also be delayed, which results in a longer melt of northern glaciers, particularly in the Yukon, where some of the largest glaciated areas are located on the planet. This delayed runoff is already causing higher than normal stream flows later in the year, as well as increased bank erosion, which adds additional sediment to streams. Increased sedimentation can be a death warrant for salmonids—particularly grayling, which are extremely sensitive to polluted water.

Increases in water temperature can also be deadly for species like grayling; once water temperatures exceed 25°C, the environment can become uninhabitable. If this happens, the range of grayling will diminish. Similarly, lake trout have a preferred water temperature of 10°C or less, so warmer water in the epilimnion (the warm surface layer in a lake that is separated by the metalimnion from the hypolimnion at the lake bottom) will drive them into colder, deeper water. This will make it more difficult to catch them by angling, and it may force them to stay in less productive water than at the surface for a longer period of time, in an area where the growing season is already short. Lake trout occur in many streams in Canada's North Country—not just lakes, as is the case south of sixty—and if these waters warm up significantly, they will no longer be habitable by this species, shrinking their overall range.

Global warming can also result in thawing of the permafrost, potentially leading to serious erosion of sediment into both lakes and streams—to the detriment of native species of fish. It can also increase the risk of wildfires, which are difficult to control in remote, northern areas. Negative side effects of wildfires include impacts on runoff, more stream bank erosion and stream sedimentation, and loss of productive riparian areas that are important in protecting watershed integrity.

In sum, global warming is causing the sea levels to rise, resulting in erosion of coastal areas that can have negative impacts on anadromous runs of Arctic char and Atlantic salmon, in particular, throughout the northern and eastern Arctic.

CHAPTER 3

ARCTIC GRAYLING: A FLY-FISHING PRIMER

by **Duane S. Radford**

According to Greek mythology, some authorities believe that the Sea King Poseidon was the god of fishes. If this is true, Poseidon could not have created a more perfect species of fish than the Arctic grayling for angling. Grayling are the glamorous beauty queens of Canada's North Country and (usually) one of the most obliging denizens of the many remote lakes and streams in northern Canada, an absolute delight to catch on lightweight spinning and fly rods.

Canada is home to what some fly fishers consider a dream fish —the Arctic grayling (*Thymallus arcticus*). As mentioned in the prior chapter, *Thymallus* is an ancient name of the grayling, pertaining to the fish's odor of thyme, which isn't necessarily always noticeable, and *arcticus*, meaning "of the Arctic."

DISTRIBUTION

A fishing trip to either the Yukon or NWT, in particular—both of which are hotbeds for this quintessential fish—would not be complete without a junket to catch grayling on a fly rod (or a spinning rod). They're also fairly common in northern British Columbia, Alberta (albeit their range has declined considerably in this province), Saskatchewan, Manitoba, and much of western Nunavut.

BIOLOGY & HABITAT

Adults migrate from ice-covered lakes and large rivers to small gravel, or rock-bottomed, tributaries during the spring breakup. Adult males are territorial on spawning grounds and will chase intruding small males. They don't build nests; rather, the eggs are simply broadcast over rocks and gravel. After spawning, adults return to their summer, autumn, and winter homes in lakes or rivers. This is typically when anglers first cue in on fishing for Arctic grayling, which are usually voracious and on the feed immediately after the spawn.

Grayling inhabit clear waters of large, cold streams and lakes in shallow water less than 3–4 m deep. Adults feed on a variety of invertebrates: aquatic insects, such as mayflies, caddis flies, and midges; terrestrial insects (bees, wasps, grasshoppers, ants, beetles); small quantities of fish; fish eggs; and even lemmings. Food studies on northern lakes indicate that terrestrial insects form the most important summer food of grayling, often comprising over half of their diet. Grayling are also opportunistic feeders, tending to school so that when you catch one, others will often be nearby. They are likewise fond of outlet streams from large lakes, especially near the mouth. These are highly productive areas and have a large quantity of aquatic insects, especially filter-feeding black fly larvae, which often literally blanket the stream bed.

FLY-FISHING TECHNIQUES: GENERAL

Arctic grayling frequent both lakes and streams in Canada's North Country; therefore, different approaches are often necessary to ensure a successful fly-fishing trip.

Catching Arctic grayling is not necessarily a slam dunk, although they're usually fairly easy to catch. Itinerant fly fishermen had best be prepared for this eventuality, remaining versatile in their fly-fishing approach. There are times when you'll have to go through your fly box before you select the right fly. Why? Because there are no sure-fire, go-to flies that I've discovered despite many years of fishing for this peacock of the ichthyological world.

Adrienne Radford with an Arctic grayling, Tincup Lake, Yukon.

The best fly fishing for grayling is during the summer and into the autumn, when it can really heat up as the fish gorge themselves in preparation for a long winter. The good news is that Arctic grayling are usually cooperative from spring to autumn. They can be hard to locate during their spring spawning season, however, due to their migratory nature. This is sometimes the case in large streams in the Yukon and Northwest Territories where they'll pull up stakes shortly after ice breakup and head for spawning streams overnight.

FISHING TECHNIQUES: RIVERS AND STREAMS

Be prepared to search out grayling using dry flies, nymphs, and streamers and have the rod and fly lines to suit such flies. This is especially the case when you're fishing remote areas in Canada's North Country. Remember the motto: *Be Prepared*. Plan for contingencies because you won't know what you're up against until you hit the water, and conditions can be highly variable. Streams may be pushing more water than normal due to the runoff and thunderstorms, or may only be a trickle of their normal flows. Cold fronts might move in and put a halt to insect hatches, or strong winds may arise and make casting a nightmare. Insect hatches are often quite sporadic throughout the range of grayling in northern Canada; consequently, it's unwise to count on ideally dry fly-fishing conditions—they often simply don't happen.

If you're after trophy fish, use a sink-tip line with a three-foot leader and put on a streamer pattern. It's seldom necessary to fish with fluorocarbon because most streams are stained with tannins and lignin from muskeg, which imparts a brown tinge to the water. Grayling are predacious fish and will attack most streamers with a vengeance, espe-

Duane Radford, fly fishing for grayling on the Sulky River, NWT.

cially large, dominant adult grayling. You'll want to fish streamers in the usual way by starting with a cast across and down runs and pools. Let the fly swing in a dead drift, twitching it from time to time to make it porpoise. Take a few steps downstream and repeat the process. I've had good results with weighted black and olive Woolly Buggers, brown and purple Conehead Woolly Buggers, and Marabou Muddler patterns. Natural patterns are the most consistent producers, not colourful, psychedelic streamers.

Should you be interested in only *catching* grayling, then Bead Head nymphs, such as the Prince Nymph and Pheasant Tail, are old standbys. Use a tapered leader with or without a strike indicator and fish the nymph in a dead drift; a strike indicator will help you see approximately where the fly is drifting. Nymphs can be very effective when insect surface activity is slow or if grayling are in swift water. If they're turned off dry flies because they've been lined too often, switch to nymphs to get back in the game. Don't laugh; this sometimes happens out of northern lodges because guides tend to take clients to the same waters again and again. Check with locals regarding go-to nymphs. In some streams, for example, the Rat Tail Special is often a choice wet fly, when other patterns don't pan out.

If you're a die-hard dry-fly enthusiast, you may be disappointed in pursuit of your quarry as insect hatches are sporadic where grayling are found; plus, fly patterns are rather limited compared with more southern standards. If there were only one or two flies of choice, they would have to be the venerable Elk Hair or Goddard Caddis, because caddis are by far the most abundant insect in northern Canadian waters inhabited by grayling. My second choice would probably be either a Brown or Grey Wulff, good imitations of the often-abundant midges in grayling water, or perhaps a Black Gnat, which imitates black flies.

Foam fly attractor patterns.

Often the best flies for grayling are foam fly attractor patterns in various colours: Turks Tarantula, Madame X, or Chernobyl Ant patterns. It's a good question how long the foam fly fad will last, but for now they're my go-to pattern when I first gear up, and can be fished all day long, regardless of whether there's a hatch underway. They also work well under all weather conditions, so stock up on foam flies and fish them with a tapered leader and a floating line. These large, gaudy patterns are usually dynamite on grayling when fished in a dead drift or skated across holding water. They can be every bit as good as the Elk Hair or Goddard Caddis, Brown and Grey Wulff patterns, or Black Gnats, and are often better because they're easier to see under poor light.

Sight cast to rising grayling or fish dry flies using a dead drift in promising holding water, mending your line as often as necessary. Don't be surprised if you can't spot any rising grayling, as it happens all the time. In terms of the size of flies, smaller is usually better, even in lightly fished lakes and streams, with the exception of foam flies and streamers where large flies are okay.

> Some fly patterns will almost consistently get strikes: *Dry flies*—Black Gnats, Elk Hair Caddis, Goddard Caddis, Brown or Grey Wulff, Royal Wulff, Red or Orange Humpys, Red or Yellow Stimulators, Black Ants; *Streamers*—Woolly Buggers and Marabou Muddlers; *Wet flies*—Black Gnats, Bead Head Prince Nymph, and Gold-Ribbed Hare's Ear searching nymphs. Use #12–16 size dry/wet fly with a 9–12' 4X leader with a short tippet with a floating or sink-tip fly line, and #6–14 streamers on a #4–5-weight fly rod to catch grayling.

TECHNIQUES: LAKES

The good news is that what works in streams also works in lakes —in spades. The only disclaimer is that if grayling are rising and you can't see any insects on the water, they're probably after emergers (emerging aquatic insects). The Klinkhåmer Special, or Klinkhamer, would be a good choice under these circumstances because of the prevalence of caddis flies in grayling waters, whether they be riverine or lentic. Typically, grayling cruise the shallows of lakes in search of something to eat. If you're fishing from a boat, you can sight cast to cruising fish if you don't see any fish rising for flies. It usually isn't necessary to troll flies in lakes to get into some action, but if you can't locate a pod, keep this tactic in the back of your mind. Some of the best fishing in lakes is found near the mouths of inlet streams where grayling congregate to capitalize on invertebrate drift that enters the still water. About the only thing that will scare them away from such areas is the sudden appearance of a lake trout with intentions of making a meal of the local grayling.

PHOTO OPS

Arctic grayling, dark colour phase, Sulky River, NWT.

When you land a grayling and want to capture the special moment with a photo, take heed of the following advice: grayling tend to be slippery and can be hard to hold. Because of this, you'll first want to wet your hands. Then, at the count of three, remove the fish from the water and rest it in the palm of your hand. Gently raise its dorsal fin by grasping it between your index finger and thumb with your free hand. Have the photographer set the fill flash on the camera in the on-position beforehand, minimizing shadow under peaked hats of the model, then put a smile on your face to record the moment—this is *the* signature picture that caps the joy of fly fishing for grayling. Above all, savour the moment. Take a few photos to make sure you get the image you want for your scrapbook, then gently release the fish to be caught another day.

CHAPTER 4

NORTHWEST TERRITORIES (NWT)

The Northwest Territories landscape is one of stark beauty that features raw wilderness with stunning vistas, mighty rivers, and immense inland lakes and dark forests where travel by bush planes is the norm. It's an exhilarating experience when a floatplane taxis from its mooring and heads into the wind. The pilot(s) will slowly push the throttle forward, and the floatplane will soon level off as it gains speed and reaches the first step on the floats. The pilot(s) may rock the plane to level it horizontally if both floats aren't lifting off the water. As the pilot pushes the throttle farther forward, the plane shudders before liftoff, rises above tree level, then the deafening sound of the motor begins to fade. The hair will rise on the back of your neck when it eventually clears the water and it wings towards your final destination.

Following the Ice North: Planning a Journey in the Northwest Territories (NWT) and Nunavut

by Chris Hanks

> CHRIS HANKS wrote the book *Fly Fishing in the Northwest Territories of Canada* (1996). He's one of the North Country's most accomplished fly fishermen, a gentle giant of a man whose deeds speak louder than his words, although he'd be too modest to ever make such a claim. He's also an outstanding fishing guide and is considered one of the most knowledgeable anglers in Canada's North Country. Chris now resides in Cripple Creek, Colorado. Co-editor Duane S. Radford was fortunate to have teamed up with Chris at Trout Rock Lodge on Great Slave Lake. In this article, Chris describes a hypothetical do-it-yourself trip based on his real-life adventures of following the spring ice breakup north, starting at the famed Kakisa River in the southern NWT, then on northwards to the mouth of the Coppermine River at Coronation Gulf in Nunavut.

The long-awaited thaw starts in late April in the southwest corner of the NWT as the Slave, Mackenzie, and Liard rivers break up, flushing ice north to the Beaufort Sea. The opening of the big rivers is driven by the tributaries that flood the Mackenzie River with fresh water, slowly releasing Great Slave Lake, Great Bear Lake, and the Arctic Ocean from winter over the next two months.

Following the ice north from the aspen-spruce forest of the south Mackenzie, along the rivers and lakes to the barren shores of Coronation Gulf in the Arctic Ocean, provides some of the best fishing the NWT and western Nunavut have to offer. The fisheries visited along the way are ancient resources that sustained the Dené and Inuit of the western Arctic long before Lt. George Back brought the first known fly rod to the NWT on the Franklin Expedition of the 1820s.

Chasing the ice north is an adventurous pursuit that occurs ahead of most fishing lodges' opening for the season, requiring research on local guides, a road trip up the Mackenzie Highway to Yellowknife, booking lodges like Trout Rock on Great Slave that open early, figuring out scheduled flights into communities like Deline on Great Bear Lake and Kugluktuk on Coronation Gulf, and arranging for accommodations. This narrative will lead you through places on the path north where all of these essentials are possible with some planning, and you will get to know the people of the northern communities as they show you this magnificent land. Particularly if you venture to Great Bear or Kugluktuk, allow yourself unstructured time to let the journey come together. People are taking time out of their lives to guide you and you need to follow their rhythm. Believe me when I tell you that it's worth the effort for the Arctic grayling, northern pike, lake trout, Arctic char, and mysterious sea-run lake trout you'll find along the way.

KAKISA RIVER ARCTIC GRAYLING

The Kakisa River provides the first harbinger of spring fishing when it breaks up in mid-April. Rising in Kakisa Lake on the Mackenzie Lowlands south of the Mackenzie Highway, it runs north over the spectacular Lady Evelyn Falls, under the highway to the MacKenzie River east of Fort Providence. During breakup, the Kakisa is big water, and early fishermen are met with blocks of ice strewn along the high clay riverbanks, ringed by spruce and still leafless aspen. The Arctic grayling are over the bar at the Kakisa's mouth on the Mackenzie River as soon as the ice moves, pushing southward against the flow of the freshet. Later in May, as the banks clear and the leaves emerge, the challenge becomes the flow of broken ice coming down from the lake. By now the grayling have settled onto gravel beds, afforded protection from the current by boulders along the bottom of the runs, staying in the river until early June when warming temperatures cause them to drop back to the cooler waters of the Mackenzie River.

During the spring run, it is seldom possible to wade clear across the river as it is fast and cold. Proper attire includes heavy neoprene waders, sometimes fitted with crampons, a stout wading staff, and heavy-duty insect repellent. Later, at the end of the run, when the waters drop and the fish start to move back downstream, it is possible to explore the river with greater ease.

Kakisa is stonefly and caddis water. During the early season freshet, the grayling are feeding on nymphs along the gravel bottom, tucked in amongst the boulders. It is necessary to get the fly down through 3–4 feet of swift water, which requires a heavy sinking tip of five or six weight line, or a long leader on a floating line with split shot. I often prefer the latter as it creates less drag; split shot can be adjusted with the addition or removal of shot.

My original success was with soft hackle partridge, as well as orange, partridge, and peacock on #12 and #14 hooks. Pushing a piece of split shot right up against the knot evolved to the use of 1/32- and 1/16-ounce jig heads painted orange or pink with a black or olive leach pattern behind the head. The rigging works well in current and emulates the soft-hackle success. Weighted golden stonefly nymphs and leaches up to about #8 also work well. Later in May and into early June, the grayling are more frequently found in mid-water and rising on hatches from caddis to midges. A parachute Adams in #14 or #16 is often useful if you do hit a hatch, but more often you take the fish on nymphs, and so I carry a range of pheasant tails (matching the size and colour becomes more important as the water clears). In early June, there is a golden stone hatch, but often by then the fish have gone downstream.

The Kakisa River is accessible by road from Edmonton, Alberta, if you are into a long road trip; fly and drive can be done from Hay River or Yellowknife, NWT. There is a day-use area near the highway crossing, which (during the run) people often use as a campsite. The NWT has a campground upriver at Lady Evelyn Falls, and hotels are available at a distance in Hay River or Fort Providence.

GREAT SLAVE LAKE PIKE

Trout Rock Lodge is located at the edge of the Canadian Shield country in the islands along the north arm of Great Slave Lake, about 12 air minutes outside Yellowknife, the capital of the NWT. Despite the close proximity, the convoluted north arm excludes local visitors. The first guests often go in by helicopter to be ready as soon as the ice moves enough that a boat can slide away from the dock.

Northern pike fishing out of Trout Rock Lodge at the old Yellowknife's Dené community of Enodah, among the islands and shallow bays of the north arm of Great Slave Lake, is never better than at ice out. Huge pike come into the warm shallow bays of this archipelago of whaleback granite islands as the ice retreats in late May and early June. Guides from the lodge will lead you into narrow back channels connecting bays known by such suggestive names as the honey hole, where "wolf packs" of pike push schools of lake whitefish into the shallows. The water boils, then they attack. Pike in the 45–48 inch range are not uncommon, with fish into the 50-plus range possible, if only because we know they have been caught there.

Eight-, nine-, or 10-weight rods are in order, and multiple rods should be strung up—one with a fast-sinking tip and the other with a dry line. Flies should be durable and easy to replicate. I use a lot of streamers made of woven strips of rabbit fur glued to the long shank of a #6 streamer hook with a large soft hackle head, all secured with a heavy brass wire rib. Yellow, chartreuse, and black strips of rabbit fur with plush hackle heads are simple but effective. A surface favourite is the baby muskrat made of woven strips of muskrat fur glued to the shank of a big streamer hook, with a large, black, soft hackle head wrapped with heavy brass wire ribbing.

Unless you're after a tippet record, I would suggest you make up 18–24 inch steel shock leaders with a high-quality ball bearing swivel/snap release to hold your fly. Loops should be fastened with stout press fitted sleeves to avoid slippage. With practice you can use a surgeon's knot to fasten the steel leader to a tapered nylon leader of 30- to 40-pound material connected to your fly line—a 4- to 6-foot leader is adequate. Beware, however, that steel leaders from commercial hardware stores don't last; the hardware isn't up to the challenge. A good snap swivel lets you change flies easily and won't straighten out the connector in a hard fight. Steel shock leaders keep you in the action and not constantly repairing frayed equipment.

Chris Hanks at Trout Rock Lodge with NWT trophy pike.

GREAT BEAR LAKE TROUT

Great Bear Lake is one of the last pristine interior "freshwater seas" in the world. With only one permanent aboriginal Slavey community at Deline—seasonally and on the western end of the Keith Arm—Trophy and Plummer's Arctic Fishing Lodges, are located on Smith Arm and Dease Arm respectively. It is a wild, untamed place; most fishermen are aware of the prize lake trout taken on tackle later in the season when Trophy and Plummer's Arctic lodges are open, but few know about the wonderful opportunity the lake provides to take lake trout on a dry fly early in the season.

July begins with the wind starting to move the ice around in the Keith Arm near the Great Bear River outlet. By the second week of July, the ice is back away from the shore, around the arm far enough to travel on the water, but it remains out in the lake to keep the waves down out on the big water.

As the ice pulls back from the mouths of creeks, the lake trout come up to feed on hatches of big-mottled brown and olive caddis that rise to the surface of the warm creek water. The best fishing is in the creek mouths along the south shore of the lake from the outlet of the Great Bear River southeast towards Grizzly Bear Mountain National Historic Site, where 8- to 12-pound fish are pretty common on the surface.

My favourite spot, locally known as Rock Creek, is located about halfway to Grizzly Bear Mountain. It's a natural break in the long boat ride to the park, and along the way, the Great Bear River has wonderful Arctic grayling fishing. The south shore is windblown with wide boulder beaches backed by willow and spruce. While not truly the barrenlands, this area sometimes feels that way.

If you've ever wondered about the giant spun-hair caddis found in older fly-pattern books, Great Bear is where you want them. My standby is the Goddard's caddis, a spun-hair pattern that can be tied onto #8–14 hooks in a variety of brown, gray, and olive mixes, each of which can be subsequently trimmed down to match the hatch. While early in the season is the best for the lake trout on the dry, the cold temperatures of Great Bear Lake mean that there are trout in the upper water column all summer, making them accustomed to a diet that includes aquatic insects as well as the more typical freshwater herring and shrimp. Later in the season, trout can be taken on stone fly nymphs, Muddler Minnows, and streamers tied on the New England-style long shaft hooks. Herring patterns, which in the good old days were made of polar bear hair, work in 10–12 feet of water on Great Bear Lake. You can fly-fish for lake trout all summer there, while in more southern climates, lake trout will have gone very deep to find cool water.

Keith Arm is not a very well-known destination, and fishing there requires taking a scheduled flight in from Norman Well to Deline. You'll find local accommodations at the Grey Goose Lodge, and you should talk with the lodge or the government of the NWT Wildlife Officer ahead of time to find a boat and guide. The lodge is across the street from the ruins of the winter quarters of the Second Franklin Expedition in 1825, which was located there to take advantage of the fishery on Great Bear Lake.

Spending time out on the lake is a real wilderness camping experience; consequently, you should be prepared for cold, windy weather and have items such as your own Mustang Floater Jacket, knee-high rubber boots, and/or insulated hip boots. Great Bear Lake will set the tone of the trip—it is big water whose moods will determine when you can travel, and when you'll drink tea and watch the waves. It's worth the trouble in your quest for big lake trout.

CORONATION GULF ARCTIC CHAR

As soon as the ice is pushed out of Coronation Gulf, summer arrives at the Arctic coast. While weather in Kugluktuk at the mouth of the Coppermine River can often be balmy in early July, Great Bear Lake to the south is still cold.

Arctic char are often elusive in the early summer as they descend the coastal rivers and move back into the ocean to follow the schools of baitfish, at which point they can often be found with binoculars along the coast. You can also search for sea birds feeding on panicking schools of capelin, churning the surface as they're chased by seals and char. The question becomes how to predictably find them.

One delightful solution is the feeding grounds around Couper Island in Coronation Gulf, which lies off the mouth of the Coppermine River near the Inuit community of Kugluktuk. Breeding char will have come back down the Coppermine River, hungry after having spawned in the inland lakes over the winter. These fish join with others that remained in the ocean over winter to feed around the islands a few miles from the community. As a result, at the height of the Arctic summer in early July, the channels around the island are full of feeding char.

A side adventure from the islands is to motor over to the mouth of the Richardson River, where you may add sea-run lake trout to your catch. These adaptable freshwater fish come down to feed in the brackish littoral zone of the river estuary and require deep-running streamers in the same baitfish patterns used for the char.

In this environment, fishing is done both from boats and from the rocky island shores, and full sinking 7–9 weight lines on rods with lots of wind-fighting backbone are recommended. You should also take a wide range of trolling streamers and steelhead flies, as it often takes some experimentation to find the right pattern. In addition, I recommend taking some black and olive heavily weighted sculpin patterns that can be bumped along the bottom.

When travelling, direct flights are available from Yellowknife to Kugluktuk, and the Coppermine Inn is one of the loveliest hotels in the north. It is normally busy, so you'll need to make reservations ahead of time, and you can find guides through the Kugluktuk Angoniatit Association (i.e., Hunters and Trappers Organization) or through the Nunavut Department of Renewable Resources.

By following the ice, there is no better end than an evening by a driftwood fire with fried char and bannock cooked over the coals in the long Arctic twilight.

CHAPTER 4 | NORTHWEST TERRITORIES

GOING NORTH

A do-it-yourself fishing trip, largely off the grid of lodge packages in the NWT and Nunavut, involves a discovery of secret places few take the time to experience. Once the north gets into your blood—and before you complete one trip—you'll find that you're planning yet another, because you likely heard about one place or another from one of your newfound Dené or Inuit friends that you simply have to see. If you dare to follow the ice breakup, you'll encounter the fish emerging hungry from a long winter under the ice—the warming water increasing their metabolism for a frenzy of summer feeding to prepare them for the next long winter—making it difficult not to stay for the entire summer.

PLUMMER'S ARCTIC LODGES: GREAT BEAR LAKE LODGE

by **Duane S. Radford**

> Ross H. Shickler really wanted to write an article about his many fishing trips (six!) on Great Bear Lake in the NWT, but failing health got in the way, so this job fell on co-editor Duane S. Radford. According to Plummer's Arctic Lodge website, Great Bear Lake boasts the "All Tackle World Records" for lake trout and Arctic grayling, as well as dozens of line class records. It is located just south of the tree line, which separates the northern boreal forest and the barren grounds. Great Bear Lake is a world-class destination for anglers, with the mother lode of trophy trout and grayling in Canada.

Plummer's Arctic Lodges is synonymous with outstanding fishing in Canada's high Arctic—particularly for trophy lake trout and Arctic grayling out of their main lodge on Great Bear Lake in the NWT—which is located in the Dease Arm in the northeast part of the lake.

The Great Bear Lake lodge is situated on the edge of the tree line just above the Arctic Circle, on an island with a causeway to the shore. Surrounded by a number of heated cabins that have separate bedrooms, hot and cold running water, showers, a sitting area, and 24-hour electricity, the main lodge features a large dining room, lounge, a gaming area, and a full-service bar.

To round out their lodge offerings in the area, you can also enjoy Trophy Lodge, which is located on Ford Bay in the Smith Arm on the west side of the lake, and the Neiland Bay Outpost on the McVicar Arm on the eastern side of the lake.

Main lodge at Great Bear Lake Lodge, NWT.

A bit farther away, you can take advantage of their lodgings on the northeast shore of Great Slave Lake, and another on the Tree River in Nunavut, located about 370 km (230 mi) northeast of the Great Bear Lake Lodge (which are all described elsewhere in this book). All trips to these lodges have been out of Yellowknife since 2009, but there are some new twists in flying to the Tree River Lodge out of Kugluktuk, Nunavut, by charter plane.

Plummer's Arctic Lodges in the NWT and Nunavut are the Holy Grail for fishermen because they boast world records for lake trout (72 pounds—1995), Arctic grayling (5.9 pounds—1967), and Arctic char (32.5 pounds—1981). Nowhere else in Canada or the United States can lay claim to this distinction; the fishing is that good, hence their claim to be the "#1 Fishing Destination in North America."

Chummy Plummer, owner of Plummer's Arctic Lodges.

It's not just the abundance of fish in Canada's Arctic, but also the sheer numbers that can be caught in a day's outing that are remarkable (although because they can be difficult to catch, Arctic char may be an exception). Without exaggeration, it's possible to catch 20-plus lake trout on a fly rod during a day without breaking much of a sweat, even with taking a couple of hours off for a delicious shore lunch. As for Arctic grayling, you actually have to give the fish a break—they're sometimes that easy to catch.

According to officials of NWT Tourism, Great Bear Lake is the largest lake entirely in Canada and it's the fourth largest lake in North America, about 150 km (95 mi) long. With a surface area of 31,328 km^2 (12,095 mi^2), an average depth of 71.7 m (235 ft), and a maximum depth of 413 m (1,355 ft), it's like being in an immense inland sea where it's impossible to see the far shoreline. Because there are untold shoals, reefs, and rocky outcrops that could sink a boat in its largely uncharted waters, it's not the sort of lake for amateur boaters, and a guided fishing trip out of Plummer's Arctic Lodges is highly recommended for safety purposes.

Plummer's Arctic Lodges runs a first-class operation, and you can obtain key information about their accommodations on their website (http://www.canadianarcticfishing.com/) and through their brochures and Information Handbook. In an interview with lodge owner Chummy Plummer, I was impressed by his down-to-earth manner and his policy to treat all guests the same, no matter their station (though he understandably made some additions to one of the cabins for security reasons during former U.S. President George H. W. Bush's visit). To sustain the world-class fishing, he has a long-standing policy of catch-and-release fishing at his lodges, save for the odd fish kept for a shore lunch. For this reason—as in the Yukon—I would encourage anglers to back off a bit and give the fish a break, because there's always a risk of some angling mortality, which increases with the overall number of fish caught.

The lodge routine begins at 7:30 a.m. with a breakfast that always features "Red River Porridge," along with other menu items. Your guide will be ready at 8:00 a.m., and shore lunches are at the request of clients—a must-do in my opinion. Dinner is served at 7:30 p.m., and by the end of the meal, you'll be ready to hit the sack and get ready for the next day's fishing—if you can get over the high-dose adrenalin rush after a good day on the water.

Duane Radford with a lake trout from Great Bear Lake.

A word of caution: the Great Bear Lake Lodge is in the high Arctic and the lake is always cold, even in the middle of summer; the ambient temperature on the water is only about 10°C during July and August, and when you factor in wind chill while speeding across the lake in a boat, it's even colder. Temperatures typically range from 10–25°C, so pack accordingly. Their handbook lists all the things you should bring, but by preparing for cold weather and dressing in layers, you should be comfortable while outside.

The lodge features various fly-outs, and a must-do trip is the Sulky River—which is a short hop from the lodge—for its legendarily large Arctic grayling. Fly-outs are on a first-come, first-served basis, so put your name in early. Grayling can be taken on spinning gear or by fly fishing in the outlet to Sulky Lake, and there are some dandies just waiting to be caught. You can also catch lake trout in the Sulky River; several were taken by clients during my trip. For another excellent jaunt, the legendary Tree River in Nunavut is a story in itself, where you can fish for its fabled Arctic char. Overall, a trip to Great Bear Lake Lodge offers unparalleled fishing for lake trout, in particular, and if you're after a real trophy, you just might connect with a new world-record fish!

As one last recommendation, be sure to spend some time in Yellowknife, the trendy and upscale capital of the NWT—also known as Canada's "Diamond Capital" for mining in the region—while on the way to one of Plummer's Arctic Lodges. A cosmopolitan city that features excellent accommodations and fine dining, it's noted for its regional cuisine, such as fresh-caught Arctic char, lake whitefish and walleye, musk ox, caribou, and bison. You'll definitely want to visit the Wildcat Café, a local historic site come modern-day eatery, as well as Bullock's Bistro, voted #1 Fish & Chips restaurant in Canada by *Reader's Digest*. Bullock's also features wild game, with caribou steaks to die for.

To take in the sights, there's a self-guided walking tour of the quirky Old Town, as well as the Northern Frontier Visitor Centre and an impressive territorial museum—the Prince of Wales Northern Heritage Centre.

Getting there is easy—airline connections between Calgary, Edmonton, and Yellowknife are excellent, with several carriers making daily flights: Air Canada, Canadian North, First Air, and WestJet. You'll be pleasantly surprised with the level of service offered by the regional carriers, which will make for a great beginning to an extraordinary trip.

FRONTIER FISHING LODGE: NWT FISHING SMORG

by **Duane S. Radford**

> I'll never forget my days on the water with fishing guide Dan Miguel out of Frontier Fishing Lodge on the east arm of Great Slave Lake about 200 km (120 air miles) east of Yellowknife. Dan is a fishing addict who doesn't seem to have any quit in his genes. He's affable, knowledgeable, and prepares a great shore lunch. The fishing for lake trout was red hot during my late-season trip, and I had some of the best fishing I've ever experienced for not only lake trout, but also for trophy-sized grayling on the Stark River, basically a stone's throw from Frontier Fishing Lodge.

Frontier Fishing Lodge is located on Great Slave Lake in the NWT and has long been a go-to destination for anglers interested in a little more variety in their adventure than many other lodges might offer in the NWT.

The fifth largest lake in North America and the tenth largest in the world, Great Slave Lake epitomizes the grandeur of the storied NWT. Trips to local fishing hotspots are sometimes measured in hours, not miles or kilometres, and you can expect to see a fairly large portion of the eastern part of the lake during a trip to Frontier Fishing Lodge.

One of the reasons the lake is dynamite for lake trout is that it's cold—these fish have a love affair with cold water, with their preferred water temperature at about 10°C. As such, you have to dress for the weather when on the water: thermal underwear, a long-sleeved shirt or pullover, waterproof pants, a jacket with a hood, a toque, and quality gloves are a must to stay warm and comfortable during a late-season trip, in particular. It can be chilly on the water even in the summer, so you'll need to dress accordingly no matter the season.

Frontier Fishing Lodge. Most lodges have all the comforts of home.

The lodge is situated near Lutsel K'e, a remote Dené Indian village on the picturesque east arm of Great Slave Lake, a short distance from the Stark River, which flows out of nearby Stark Lake. Lutsel K'e was formerly known as "Snowdrift" but had an official name change in 1992.

Owner Wayne Witherspoon purchased the lodge in 1990, and it has always been a family operation. It had been a dream of Wayne's late brother, Warren—who died in 1987 after living his dream for seven years—to own and operate a fishing lodge. His other brother, Wes, who lives in Calgary, Alberta, Canada, is a silent partner, although he visits the lodge occasionally. Witherspoon's lovely wife Debbie is also a driving force behind day-to-day lodge operations.

A full-service establishment with log cabins (you don't even have to make your bed; chambermaids take care of that), it also features single rooms within the lodge, along with a recreation room, hot and cold running water, a full-service bar, and an experienced chef, with all the amenities of home.

Dan Miguel making a shore lunch—a highlight of trips to Northern Canada—on Great Slave Lake.

Witherspoon says that the lake trout fishing on Great Slave Lake is second to none, and that he doesn't believe there's a place anywhere in the world that surpasses it in terms of size and numbers. He adds that Great Bear Lake boasts having bigger fish, and concedes that they do, but says that nobody catches as many fish—or betters the average size they catch—as they do on Great Slave Lake. "Out of this cold water they're exceptionally good eating," Witherspoon says, and I'd have to agree with his claims after having feasted on some lake trout shore lunches prepared by my affable fishing guide, Dan Miguel.

His soft-spoken nature may be a little beguiling, but Witherspoon isn't stretching the truth about the fantastic fishing at Frontier Fishing Lodge. I found that out by fishing the hard way—using a fly rod—on a fishing trip for lake trout and Arctic grayling during an early September outing just before the lodge closed for the season. I wanted to experience the challenge of catching lake trout and grayling on a fly rod, rather than with conventional spinning and casting tackle, and while a fly rod is a definite handicap when tackling large lake trout, I actually had my guide looking over his shoulder one afternoon when I out-fished him three to one for a spell. You'll catch fish—lots of fish—and some real brutes, using either a fly rod, spinning, or casting rod out of Frontier Fishing Lodge; bringing in 20 lake trout a day is normal during the season, without exaggeration.

Witherspoon shares that the fishing for Arctic grayling in Great Slave Lake is also exceptional compared with anywhere in the world. The average size of grayling is at least two pounds, and they run about 16–18 inches, with some reaching 24 inches and four pounds. He adds that they also have incredible northern pike fishing, but only in early or late season. In mid-summer you simply can't find those big guys.

While all three species are available, the big draw continues to be the lake trout. People seek the chance of catching one up to 50 pounds, and the lodge offers them that opportunity, even providing heavy-duty fishing gear for those who need it.

I travelled to Yellowknife by First Air from Edmonton, Alberta, Canada, and barely had time to finish an in-flight breakfast and read the paper before the plane landed. I stayed at the Chateau Nova—an upscale hotel in downtown Yellowknife—where the fish chowder and grilled pickerel were superb. The free shuttle between the airport and the hotel was a nice touch, and there was another free shuttle from the Chateau Nova to the Air Tindi floatplane base on Great Slave Lake that ferried the other guests and me to the lodge in a Twin Otter floatplane. (Air Tindi is a large, local carrier out of Yellowknife that schedules and charters air service throughout the Yukon, NWT, and Nunavut with a fleet of aircraft on floats, wheels, and skis.)

A fully modern city with all the amenities of settled Canada—paved roads, street lights, city buses, and lots of places to shop and dine—Yellowknife is a wonderful place to stay. With plenty of good accommodations, and with all the different kinds of fish on the menus, you'd swear you were on the coast.

I'm usually a bit skeptical when I hear stories about fabulous fishing from lodge owners or read articles about how great the fishing is at a particular lodge, but as I already described, this one does not disappoint. You can purchase your fishing licence either at the lodge or in town at the local visitor centre. Canadian visitors to the NWT can purchase a seasonal visitor's licence for $20, or a three-day licence for $15. Non-residents of Canada pay $40 for a seasonal licence, $30 for a three-day licence.

Dan Miguel, Frontier Fishing Lodge guide, with a Great Slave Lake lake trout.

There's a saying that "Everything is big in Texas." While I'm not aware of any such saying for the NWT, my impression is that everything would be even bigger in this corner of the world. Nature is on a grand scale in the NWT; I've always felt somewhat overwhelmed during my trips to this northern frontier. It is truly a land of giants—with awesome lakes, rivers, landscapes, and fish, surrounded by majestic escarpments, brooding forests, and primeval raw beauty, making it a place of mystery and solitude.

If you're an adventurer, you'll meet your match in the NWT and be humbled in the process. The vistas near Redcliff Island (located west of Frontier Fishing Lodge) are absolutely stunning with towering, jagged cliffs of granite rising several hundred feet out of the water.

The same can be said for the scenery around Pearson Point, Fortress Island, and The Gap (to the north of the lodge).

IF YOU GO: Contact Frontier Fishing Lodge

Toll-Free: 1-877-465-6843 **Telephone**: (780) 466-3874 (From June 8 to September 10, telephone the lodge at (867) 370-3501)

E-mail: frontierfishinglodge.com/contact-us

Website: www.frontierfishinglodge.com

By Mail: P.O. Box 32008, Edmonton, Alberta, Canada, T6K 4C2

During my trip to Frontier Fishing Lodge, I felt that I'd earned my Order of Arctic Adventurers, North of 60 Chapter certificate (of this organization), for "having demonstrated the initiative, integrity and bold adventurous spirit of the true Arctic explorers who have crossed the 60th Parallel hereafter being recognized as an honourable member."

Plummer's Arctic Lodges: Great Slave Lake

by Duane S. Radford

Plummer's Arctic Lodges Great Slave Lake Lodge is located in the east arm of Great Slave Lake about 240 km (150 mi) east of Yellowknife. The east arm has been compared metaphorically with a studio for Canada's famed Group of Seven world-renowned landscape artists, and rightly so. The scenery surrounding the east arm is absolutely stunning, and fishing in the Taltheilei Narrows (Dené for "the place of open water") where the lodge is located should be on every angler's bucket list—you just know you're going to hook a trophy lake trout in the narrows as the current rushes underneath your fishing boat.

The big lake trout hit my streamer hard, and I responded with a solid tug on my line to set the hook. The battle was on as I reeled the fish towards the boat. Things started off okay, and it appeared I had the fish under control, but this trout behaved like a large fish and was soon having its way with me, peeling off fly line at will. I was well into my backing as the fish made yet another beeline for deep water when the leader snapped—argh! Upon later inspection, the 20-pound leader appeared shredded as I shook my head in despair. I had no doubt just lost a monster trout in the Taltheilei Narrows on Great Slave Lake in the NWT—it seemed there was simply too much tension on the leader, and it frayed at the worst possible moment in the lake's ice-cold waters.

Booked into Plummer's Arctic Lodges Great Slave Lake Lodge in August, 2009, my wife Adrienne and I were eager to enjoy some late-season fishing for lake trout on a fly rod. Our planning for the trip began at the Edmonton Boat & Sportsmen Show the previous March, after speaking with Grant Nolan who manages the lodge and had done so for the previous 25 years at the time. Grant is one of those positive, high-energy people who radiates enthusiasm, and after he described the lodge and the outstanding fishing opportunities, my old buddy, Don Meredith, and I decided to book a trip with our wives. Neither Adrienne nor Don's wife Betty had ever been to the NWT, and as things turned out, the trip was a huge adventure for them. Don had been to the NWT before as a consulting biologist, having worked in the high Arctic; I had been there several times. I've always been in awe of the landscape, where man's footprint is still pretty light—it's big country with spectacular scenery and giant fish.

Great Slave Lake Lodge, NWT.

Great Slave Lake Lodge is part of Canada's iconic Plummer's Arctic Lodges chain and has been a long-standing destination of itinerant fishermen from around the globe. Plummer's also has three other lodges on Great Bear Lake, as well as the famed Tree River Lodge near Coronation Gulf on the Arctic Ocean. Clients travel by chartered, wheeled aircraft from Yellowknife to a gravel runway just north of the Great Slave Lake lodge, and then are ferried in an old school bus to their quarters.

Once you arrive at the lodge, you don't even have to touch your luggage. You're housed in cozy cabins with full room service; in fact, towels are changed more often than in any hotel I've stayed. The cabins have comfortable beds and full bathroom facilities with hot and cold running water and 24-hour electricity. A carafe of steaming hot coffee is brought to your door at 6:30 a.m., and breakfast is served in the main lodge at 7:30 a.m. Clients meet their guide at the dock at 8:00 a.m. to start the day's fishing.

After the morning excursion, a not-to-be-missed shore lunch of epic proportions is served at about 1:00 p.m. in a secluded spot. If you can keep your eyes open after this pagan feast, you can fish until 5:30 p.m., when you'll return to the lodge to be greeted by ice in your room for a beverage before your 7:30 dinner—featuring prime rib, roast turkey, ribs, and barbecued strip loin steaks. Forget your diet—you won't shed any weight at this lodge! Desserts are great, especially the carrot cake, and the lodge has full bar service as well. You can also run up a tab at the main lodge and tackle shop.

Plummer's Great Slave Lodge features outstanding fishing, especially for large lake trout. There are so many Arctic grayling in the shallows near the lodge that you don't even have to leave camp to catch them. Pike are apparently a bit harder to find near the lodge, but no matter—during my trip, over a dozen lake trout were taken that topped 20 pounds, with the largest weighing over 40 pounds. Most of these large trout were caught with bait-casting rods and reels with king-size jigs, spoons, and flatfish—which the lodge supplies—using conventional fishing techniques in water up to 40-plus feet deep.

Located within a proposed new national park on the east arm of Great Slave Lake—an area that boasts awesome, legendary Canadian Group of Seven picturesque scenery—the lodge is surrounded by untold numbers of lakes, primal brooding forests, sheer granite cliffs that soar some 500 feet above the water's edge, and never-ending jagged escarpments cloaked with stark, black spruce. It's a land of haunting beauty, quiet and pristine. The area has a colourful history, heralded by English explorer Samuel Hearne, who was the first European to see Great Slave Lake in the winter of 1771. Fort Reliance is located on the far northeastern shore of the lake and was established in 1833 as winter headquarters for the Arctic overland expeditions in search of the John Ross expedition led by George Back. It is also the site of an annual gathering during the first week of August of local Dené First Nations peoples, who meet to celebrate their local traditions near the Lockhart River, a gateway to ancestral hunting grounds on the barrens to the north of Great Slave Lake.

The history of Plummer's Arctic Lodges dates back to 1938 when Warren C. Plummer and his father, Chummy, ventured some 150 miles (240 km) from Yellowknife by canoe to what would later become the site of the Great Slave Lake lodge in 1949. Warren's son, also named Chummy, currently heads up Plummer's Arctic Lodges out of Winnipeg, Manitoba, Canada. The lodge is located at the Taltheilei Narrows, a pinch point in the east arm of the lake, and features strong currents that attract baitfish, which are prey for lake trout. Water flows from numerous rivers into this arm of the lake, which creates a veritable riptide as it rushes through the Taltheilei Narrows. In fact, the current is so strong that there's open water in the narrows during the winter. The narrows are quite unusual and have been known to feature currents running in two different directions at the same time.

According to officials of NWT Tourism, Great Slave Lake—named after the Slavey Indians—is 480 km (300 mi) long and 19–109 km (12–68 mi) wide. It is the second largest lake in the NWT after Great Bear Lake and covers an area of 28,568 km^2 (11,030 sq mi). It is one of the deepest lakes in the world at 614 metres (2014 feet) and very cold, translating into near-perfect habitat for lake trout, which have a preferred water temperature of 10°C.

One of the local fishing guides, Yellowknife native Sean Root, says that the lake trout don't behave in their usual manner in Great Slave Lake—normally they retreat to cold water during the heat of the summer, but in Great Slave Lake, the trout are often near the top, and downriggers aren't required. This is good news for fly fishermen because lake trout can be taken with a fly in the top 10–15 feet of water during the open water season. Mind you, our fishing guide, Garrett Braun of Fisher Branch in Manitoba, Canada, marked a lot of trout on the bottom at 30–40 feet, so jigging certainly has its place, and perhaps the largest of trout hang out in deeper water. What surprised me was that we

consistently caught as many lake trout on a fly as did the other parties at the lodge who used hardware, although they did catch the largest trout. We were the only party who was fly fishing during our trip, and on our best days, we enjoyed double-digit catches—even though we always had a long, leisurely shore lunch—which was a testament to the great fishing.

Great Slave Lake is divided into various special management areas, and Area VI in the east arm has special restrictions for lake trout: the daily catch limit is one, and it may not be more than 70 cm (28 inches), or fork length. Regardless, Plummer's Arctic Lodges has long

had a policy of catch-and-release fishing and only allows guests to keep trout for a shore lunch. They even feature a "Hug and Release" trademark on their brochures and correspondence. As such, barbless hooks are mandatory in the NWT.

Lodge manager Grant Nolan is originally from Edmonton, Alberta, Canada, and is based at Plummer's Arctic Lodges headquarters in Winnipeg, Manitoba. He used to own a restaurant in Edmonton until Garry Powers, who formerly managed the Great Slave Lodge, walked into the establishment one day and invited Grant to the lodge for the summer. As the saying goes: the rest is history—he's been managing the lodge ever since. "Once you've been here, it's really hard to back away from it," Grant chuckled during an interview.

He receives particular joy from the people who visit the lodge —he relishes seeing the happy faces on the dock, and he's not discouraged by the occasional sad ones, because he knows he can always make things better for them on the water. Though the opening and closing of the lodge both require a lot of work, and he must ultimately wear a lot of different hats—including running the grader on the runway, the caterpillar, and other pieces of machinery—he says there's really nothing he dislikes about his job.

While the lodge itself provides a lovely respite, the key attraction is the fishing, which Grant says is probably as good as he's seen anywhere for lake trout. With the scenery second to none in the world, the surroundings are breathtaking, and the staff is so friendly that everybody who stays there will cherish it as a lasting memory.

We booked with First Air—a regional carrier that boasts first-class service, bar none—for our flights from Edmonton, Alberta, to Yellowknife, and Joel Maillet from Plummer's Arctic Lodges met us at the airport upon our arrival to ensure all of our needs were addressed. There is a free shuttle service from the airport to the hotel, but we opted to spend a pleasant afternoon in Yellowknife. We purchased our fishing licences at the Northern Frontier Visitor Centre, which features several North Country interpretive displays, bought souvenirs, did some shopping and sightseeing in town, had scrumptious bison burgers at the Wildcat

Café local historic site, and enjoyed comfortable quarters in The Explorer Hotel.

In planning your trip, keep in mind that the lodge usually opens on June 20 and closes around the end of August, but it has operated until the end of September on occasion. Full capacity is 44 people, and clientele come from all over the world, as far away as Australia. Each of Plummer's lodges is unique, and visitors will enjoy a totally different experience at each one. If you're looking for a premier getaway trip with action-packed fishing, include Plummer's Great Bear Lake Lodge on your bucket list.

IF YOU GO: Contact Plummer's Arctic Lodges (http://www.canadianarcticfishing.com/) for details regarding lake trout fishing in the NWT. Check out the spectacular NWT Tourism website (http://www.spectacularnwt.com/) for vacation planning in the Land of the Midnight Sun.

Great Slave Lake Lodge boats.

TASTE OF ARCTIC PIKE FISHING: TROUT ROCK LODGE, NORTHWEST TERRITORIES

by Duane S. Radford

> Ross H. Shickler said there had to be at least one chapter in this book about the outstanding fishing for pike in Canada's North Country. These are not your ordinary pike; they're literally MONSTERS—actually scary they're so large—unmatched in size anywhere else in North America. Located in the north arm of Great Slave Lake, Trout Rock Lodge is one of the best spots for trophy pike North of Sixty. Their website boasts, "Trout Rock Lodge offers the best damned trophy pike fishing on the planet. Guaranteed!" Now, that's no small claim, but entrepreneurial lodge owner Ragnar Wesstrom could be right!

Trout Rock Lodge is named after a local Dené Indian landmark in the north arm of Great Slave Lake in the NWT and is renowned for monster pike. I've enjoyed some of the best pike fishing I've experienced in Canada at the "Rock," as the lodge is known locally, and prior to my trip, I was pumped up before I even left home, as lodge owner Ragnar Wesstrom told me they were having unbelievable fishing, with guests catching 30–40 pike—several over 40 inches—every day!

Trout Rock is the only lodge in the north arm of Great Slave Lake—the fifth largest freshwater lake in North America—a lodge Ragnar built from scratch starting in 1991. It specializes in northern pike fishing, some of which have been known to top 50 inches in length. But that's not the whole story, by any means. The rest is really about a taste of Arctic fishing, as this lodge offers what is probably one of the most accessible pike waters in the NWT, and about the adventure of a fly-in fishing trip in Canada's

North Country, something ordinary folks only dream about for the most part. With today's convenient air connections, it's no longer merely a dream; it's within easy reach of the travelling sportsman. If you prefer to drive to the NWT, well, that's another option.

> Make sure you're covered for an air ambulance by your local health plan before you venture north (just in case of an emergency) or purchase insurance with an agency such as MedjetAssist (http://medjetassist.com/ or call 800-5ASSIST), which provides coverage for not only the United States, but for Canada as well.

Trout Rock Lodge, NWT.

Trout Rock Lodge is located on an island in Great Slave Lake, only a 12-minute floatplane ride from Yellowknife—the bustling, modern capital of the NWT with a population of about 20,000 in 2013. Yellowknife is the Diamond Capital of North America™ and has been called a cosmopolitan outpost in the wilderness. Named after aboriginals who carried copper knives, it has numerous modern amenities: paved roads, streetlights, buses, shopping centres, great accommodations, and fine dining. I enjoyed a famous 'bou burger (caribou) in the historic Wildcat Café and a buffalo ribeye at the Oldtown Landing restaurant—signature meals in Canada's northern frontier—before departing for the "Rock." Be sure to enjoy a Yellowknife walkabout and visit the local attractions, which are real treats.

Once at the "Rock," be prepared to see huge pike, which are cooperative and can be caught by fly fishing or spin casting. Ragnar recommends a 9-weight fly rod, big streamers, steel leaders, floating and sink-tip lines for fly fishermen; I used an 8-weight rod with both floating and sink-tip lines. A large arbor reel is a must for trophy pike; for spin fishing, Ragnar recommends at least a 20-pound test line, along with Rapala Weedless Minnows, Doctor Spoon, Johnson's Silver Minnow, and Williams Wabbler lures, as well as other popular pike lures. Streamers, spoons, crank baits, jigs, and spinners will all catch fish.

In the Land of the Midnight Sun, the sun never sets in the summer, and it's actually light enough to read a newspaper at midnight at the "Rock." The long days are absolutely invigorating, and if they don't make you feel young again, probably nothing will.

To get to Yellowknife—the jumping-off base for most Arctic fishing adventures, which has a plethora of floatplanes—you can take the Mackenzie Highway from Edmonton to Yellowknife (1,513 km) if you would rather drive on a paved road than fly. There are several daily flights in and out of Yellowknife by commercial carriers—I took a flight with Canadian North out of Edmonton, Alberta, Canada, and was in Yellowknife in one and a half hours. A subsequent short charter flight on Air Tindi—The North's Family Airline—in a Twin Otter, quickly brought me to the lodge. If you're searching for ways to travel by air to the NWT and get around once you arrive, check out the following website for further details:

www.nwt.worldweb.com/Transportation/Airlines/

> Fishing regulations for the NWT can be obtained online at the following website: http://bit.ly/nwtwildlife. Visit the territorial tourism website or dial up their call centre below where you can make an online or telephone request for a travel brochure and/or travel planner. If you're interested in vacation opportunities, visit www.explorenwt.com or call 1-800-661-0788. You can "Live the Legend" in the "Land of the Midnight Sun," which is the motto of the NWT.

So, what's the routine at Trout Rock Lodge? Breakfast is served at 8:00 a.m. and dinner at 7:00 p.m., with guests having the option of sandwiches for lunch, or a shore lunch prepared by the fishing guides. Fishing starts at around 9:00 a.m. and runs until about 6:00 p.m. The lodge features primarily 18' Crestliner "John boats," which are ideal for casting—especially off the casting deck on the bow for fly fishermen—with quiet, 40-horsepower Yamaha outboard motors. All trips are guided, and boats usually travel in pairs for safety. Guides have two-way radios and are familiar with boating hazards, taking great care while navigating in the shallow north arm.

Fishing occurs amid an archipelago surrounding the "Rock" with numerous islands, bays, channels, reefs, and boulder gardens —ideal pike habitat. All fishing is with single, barbless hooks and only a few small pike may be kept for a shore lunch—it's all catch and release otherwise. "Small" is a relative term for pike in the north arm of Great Slave Lake, meaning less than about three feet long! Be prepared for brutish pike, and gear up accordingly because they're very hard on tackle—they'll snap lines, break rod tips, straighten swivel snaps, bust wire leader swivels, and destroy reels. If you're fly fishing, be sure to pack an extra fly rod and reel. Personally, I prefer Titanium rather than wire leaders when fly fishing for pike, and I recommend packing foul-weather gear in case the weather is bad, which won't turn off the fish or keep you in camp because of all the protected areas to go fishing near the lodge.

IF YOU GO: For more information about Trout Rock Lodge and their facilities (or a brochure) contact:

Ragnar Wesstrom at Enodah Wilderness Travel Ltd. Box 2382, Yellowknife, NWT, X1A 2P8, Canada.

Phone: (867) 873-4334; **Fax**: (867) 873-3825

E-mail: monsterpike@enodah.com

Website: www.enodah.com

Duane Radford with a northern pike at Trout Rock Lodge.

Having had a taste of Arctic fishing at Trout Rock Lodge, I would definitely like to go back for second helpings! It really is a hot-spot where you have a legitimate chance of topping the 50-inch mark for pike, without any exaggeration. I lost track of how many pike I landed that topped 40 inches—there were that many —and my best pike taped out at 49 inches.

THE BUZZ ABOUT MOSQUITO LAKE

by Tom Adamchick

> Tom Adamchick is a field editor, columnist, and former fly-fishing editor for *Outdoor Canada* and has long been hooked on fishing out-of-the-way lakes and streams in Canada's North Country. Tom, who lives in Ontario, has been a member of the Canadian Fly-Fishing Team and is a modern-day Indiana Jones of the fly-fishing community. Mosquito Lake is located in the heart of the NWT, east of Great Slave Lake, and features outstanding fishing for trophy lake trout in particular. For giant lakers on the fly, this remote NWT destination promises exciting ice-out action—and a taste of living on the edge.

When I fly in the North off the routine commercial air routes, I keep a photocopied page from an atlas on my lap. I like knowing where I am, so I use it to reference the landmarks below. On this trip, the last traces of road and trail petered out less than two hours north of my departure point in Winnipeg, with the thick carpet of black spruce and jack pine interrupted only by countless lakes and streams. My final destination was Tukto Lodge on trout-filled Mosquito Lake, which lies just north of the treeline in the Northwest Territories and south of the fabled Thelon River.

The first stop, though, was the sand airstrip at Kasba Lake—1,200 km (745 mi) north of Winnipeg, Manitoba—where I left the 52-seat Convair 580 and transferred to a Beaver for the final, 400-km (248-mi) leg. At Beaver altitude, I could see that the stands of trees were gradually thinning, giving way to rock and sandy outcrops, the ridges and humps collecting caribou tracks that spread out in myriad sandy roadways. If I hadn't kept reminding myself where I was, I could have believed I was looking down at rough golf courses with endless sand traps.

Then the tree clumps disappeared altogether and suddenly we were cruising over the barrens, an endless tract of gravel, bog lakes, and ponds with scattered stunted trees and rock, and, every once in a while, a snowbank—on July 18th at that. Just to see this country from the air made the trip worthwhile. Not that I was in the North merely for the scenery, mind you.

No, my goal over the next four days was quite straightforward: to catch monster ice-out lake trout on the fly, and to put both my skills and my gear to the test.

As we reached Mosquito Lake, I soon spied Tukto Lodge, with its small, white buildings perched atop moss, bracken, wildflowers, and ancient Precambrian Shield. Tukto is the only fishing camp on the 970 square-kilometre (375 square-mile) lake, which has long had a reputation for serving up trophy lakers as big as 50 pounds. It's on the same parallel as Yellowknife and Rankin Inlet, smack dab between them, nearly 500 km (310 mi) each way. Lodge owner Bob Huitikka keeps the fishing pressure low through a catch-and-release policy, although some small fish are kept for shore lunches. He also takes in fewer than 100 anglers during the six-week, ice-free season at Mosquito Lake and a sister operation on nearby Dubawnt Lake in Nunavut, where he runs three outpost camps.

Not surprisingly, then, Tukto Lodge is small and personal, where roughing it entails a great dining room, cozy cabins, and other amenities you'd expect at a top-quality facility. There is even Internet access. I appreciated everything all the more considering the distance it had to travel to get there. And the weather? A warm 28°C, while the ice-out water was a frigid 6°C, keeping the trout in the shallows. Perfect.

Almost as soon as my assigned cabin mate and fly-fishing partner, Eugene Fox from Colorado, and I got checked in, we hit the water with guide Mike Myslicki to get acclimatized and do some fishing. I had assumed we'd be fishing out in the huge expanse of the open lake—just like in those NWT tourism photos we've all seen. Wrong. Instead, we headed to a narrow outflow with rushing water. Luckily, Fox and I both had heavy flies to heave at the choice spots.

My first trout struck within five minutes, slicing my fly line through the water every which way until I began the retrieve. It soon became a game of gain two feet, lose one, as I winched in the line, battling both the fish and the current. Coupled with a sink-tip line, my 5-weight rod may have got the size 4 silver Clouser Minnow to the right place, but as a fighting tool it was nearly outmatched by the 24-inch laker in fast water. After finally releasing my catch, I knew it was time to switch to my 9-weight gear. What's comfortable for playtime in eastern Ontario and western Quebec just doesn't cut it in the rushing waters of the NWT.

Next, Myslicki moved us to the head of the rapids and anchored. In less than an hour, Fox and I landed five fish ranging from 18 to 24 inches, all on streamers. Then Myslicki pulled anchor again and we slid down to the tail of the rapids, spooking a gigantic golden eagle fishing from a partially submerged rock. Within a few minutes, Fox was into three Arctic graylings, one after another, the largest of which was 18 inches. At any one time, roughly 100 caddis flies were doing their characteristic figure-eight mating flight just over the surface. Every once in a while, a snout would emerge from the depths and there'd be one less dancer. By the end of our first day, I wasn't sure if the fishing could possibly get much better.

Day two's adventure was on an unnamed river draining Mary's Lake west of camp. My first lake trout sucked in a size 2 white Bunny Leech. This fish frightened me. I knew in my gut there was serious mass at the end of the line, unlike anything I'd caught the day before. Then there was the raging torrent, the drifting boat, and massive submerged boulders to contend with.

Fighting a large fish is a head game demanding attitude, strategy, and the occasional bluff. But this trout had a mind of its own—and we were in its territory. Once the giant decided to move, it simply sauntered upstream as we drifted farther down, forcing me to stingily give out line. I eventually convinced the fish to turn its head to the side, just enough to get it to lumber calmly down alongside the boat. Then it saw us, and all hell broke loose.

As the trout panicked and shifted into overdrive, I imagined the fly line wrapping around the toothy boulders or snagging on the prop. And when the fish lunged from one sheltering rock to another, my boat mates and I shifted our positions accordingly. This in-boat square dance happened three times over a period of five minutes, but once we drifted into the tail-out of the rapids, I was able to wrestle the lunker to the side of the boat.

It stretched the tape at 37 inches, breaking my personal record for a laker on a fly—and it was only our second day. If the fish had been any bigger, I would have only been along for the ride. My graphite rod had felt as though it was going to explode from the load at least twice, and it was remarkable the line didn't snag.

Tom Adamchick caught this lake trout on a fly at Mosquito Lake.

After that, we followed up with seven more lake trout ranging from 20 to 27 inches, then kept two small fish for shore lunch on a small, wind-battered island. As there was no wood of any kind for burning, Myslicki served one of his patented laker lunches prepared over the propane stove we brought along. Meanwhile, hordes of blackflies coasted to our lee out of the wind, and I spent a fair amount of time inside my bug jacket to avoid giving them a chance for a meal.

On closer examination, however, I was happily surprised to discover that about 80 percent of the blackflies were actually chironomids, small caddis, and tiny stonefly adults. No wonder I didn't get chewed to bits when I wasn't wearing my bug jacket. Most of this crowd was friendly, and without teeth. Around Tukto, the biting bugs are all but gone by the end of July.

Not that that should have been surprising—what occurs over six months at home in the south takes just six weeks in this treeless expanse. When we first arrived, for example, white wildflowers were in bloom; by day two they were finished. Geologist Gord Davidson, who was leading a uranium exploration crew based at Tukto, warned me the land would get under my skin. And he should know, having first walked throughout the area in the early 1970s, staking his claims.

There are other natural wonders too. In August, it's common to see anywhere from 1,000 to 10,000 caribou from the 200,000-strong Beverly herd come through during migration. And Joe Markham, one of the hardware-chucking guests at camp, got a photo of a musk ox at close range beside one of the fishing hotspots. The encounter ended with a snort.

A REMARKABLE PIECE OF REAL ESTATE, INDEED

When the fishing is great, you can get blasé about watching porpoising lakers as they surface feed. You might even pass them up in your quest for the big trophy fish that are supposed to be farther downstream. So it was that our destination for the third day was the second rapids along the outflow to the east, where another group had caught six fish in the 30-pound range the day before. But talk about conjuring up bad fishing karma.

After a few attempts to anchor in the middle of the 150-yard torrential rapids, we finally managed to hold our place in the relative sanctuary behind a boulder. But the swirling water just toyed with our fly lines, and to make the situation even more challenging, the best holding lies were directly beneath or beside the boat.

Every few moments, we'd see 30-pounders and larger ambling along in the much calmer water below the fast conveyer belt above them—there was no way any fly line was going to penetrate that. Trolling the currents downstream from the anchored boat yielded three 18- to 28-inchers, but seeing those lumbering lunkers at our feet was frustrating. Oh, to have had spinning gear.

After finally giving up, we drifted into some quieter riffles where we could hear the sloppy sipping sounds of grayling feeding on stranded caddis and midges. Within a few minutes, our 5-weight outfits had pulled in eight feisty 12- to 19½-inchers on dark dry flies for short fights and quick releases beside the boat. I also waded in calmer water and released at least another 10 grayling within 15 minutes.

Later, as we prepared for shore lunch, Fox and I checked the stomach contents of our small lake trout keepers. There were no baitfish, which I found surprising, but they were jammed full of adults and pupae of chironomids, blackflies, and caddis. Fox figured the opportunistic lakers were keying in on the high-fat bugs and saving the baitfish and minnows for the much longer and leaner bug-free times. As Fox was once a biochemistry professor at the Universities of Wisconsin and Kansas and has vast scientific knowledge, I trusted his analysis.

After lunch, which a gyrfalcon also attended, we trolled and picked up fish along the shores of another unnamed lake upriver towards camp. At the mouth of the river, the morning sippers were still at it, and in no time we had several 18- to 30-inch trout. Our good karma had returned.

On our fourth and final day on the water—it was 24°C and not too windy—we decided to explore Mosquito Lake itself. The western shore had huge sandstone bluffs and adjacent plains that looked as though they'd been grazed to a perfectly even height. The scene had the look of an Irish summer landscape, except for the snowbanks. We also spotted an old trapper's shack, which was just begging to be explored.

The story goes it was built around 1946—about the time my 37-inch laker was just a small fry—by one Fred Riddell, a recluse who settled in the area after the war, disgusted with mankind. Apparently he had dragged the timbers in from a sheltered ravine about a mile away to build his isolated redoubt. And he couldn't have picked a better spot, with Mosquito Lake marking the end of the permafrost, its southern end fringed with scattered dwarf black spruce. To the east, west, and north, meanwhile, lies nothing but bald barrens.

Looking back, I'm thankful I got to see the area the way it is now. The surrounding geology is attracting uranium and diamond exploration, while out-of-control fuel prices threaten to put a damper on future recreational travel. Without question, Mosquito Lake is on the edge, both geographically and metaphorically. And not only did I see an amazing part of the world, I also accomplished what I had come to do: experience the thrill of catching giant, wild lake trout on the fly.

GETTING THERE: The adventure starts at Winnipeg's International Airport or, more accurately, at the Four Points by Sheraton Hotel, mere steps from the airport. An early-morning charter flight to Kasba Lake, followed by a floatplane ride, gets you to Tukto Lodge, the only camp on Mosquito Lake, around noon.

ACCOMMODATIONS: Tukto Lodge can house up to 18 anglers in its three comfortable, heated cabins with hot running water and most of the amenities of home. On-site staff prepare great meals in the new lodge headquarters, which includes a kitchen, dining room, common area, cash bar, and tackle shop. Shore lunches are hearty, and the guides try to outdo each other in creative ways to prepare lake trout.

WHEN TO GO: Right after ice-out, usually during the second week of July through to freeze-up in late August, depending on the weather. Even that far north, however, climate change is making a difference—for the past few years, ice-out has arrived a week earlier than normal.

PERMITS: NWT fishing licences are available at the camp.

GEAR: Single barbless hooks are mandatory. For lake trout, an 8- or 9-weight fly rod setup is ideal. Bring various lines for different depths and, of course, your reel should be smooth enough to handle very large fish. Try the likes of sizes 2–6 Woolly Buggers, Rabbit Strip Leeches, and Muddler Minnows. For Arctic grayling, a 5- or 6-weight rod with floating and sink-tip line is all that's necessary; throw dries such as Royal Wulffs, Elk Hair Caddis, and other stimulators in sizes 10–14. Spin fishermen will want 20-pound-test line with 4½-inch spoons, such as Dardevles or Len Thompson spoons, for the lake trout. For grayling, #0 or #1 spinners, such as the Mepps Black Fury, are good bets on ultra light tackle.

CLOTHING: Think cold—10 to 20°C—wet and windy. That's the average, so it can get nastier. Insulated clothing, warm footwear, a hat, and gloves are essential. The lodge provides a complete list of recommended clothing and gear: trust it.

MORE INFORMATION: Tukto Lodge, 1-800-760-0924; www.arcticfishing.com. NWT Tourism, 1-800-661-0788; www.explorenwt.com

AUTHOR'S NOTE

The real "RIDDLE" behind the Mystery Trapper's shack: "The Buzz about Mosquito Lake" (October/November) brought back many memories. The article suggested Fred Riddle was a hermit. However, he was not a recluse, nor disgusted with mankind, but merely a solitary trapper. My wife and I knew him well as he visited us in Fort Smith, NWT, and I, as part of my duties with the Canadian Wildlife Service, brought his mail and supplies while on his trapline. He came north to trap in 1929, starting along the Dubawnt River north from Stony Rapids, Saskatchewan. Later he established his base camp in the southwestern corner of Mosquito Lake where he stored lake trout and whitefish for his dog team. He also had an out cabin in a sandy area southwest of Mosquito Lake, and he built a log cabin on the Thelon River.

—*Letter to the Editor submitted by the late Ernie Kuyt, Edmonton, Alberta, Canada (reprinted with permission of* Outdoor Canada*).*

CHAPTER 5

Nunavut

A River Charmed: Nunavut's Tree River
by Duane S. Radford

Of all the rivers and streams I've fished in Canada, not one has been as challenging as the remote Tree River that flows into the Arctic Ocean—it is the Everest for fly-fishers in particular (and I've fished across Canada from coast to coast to coast). Many fine anglers have met their Waterloo on the Tree River and gone home skunked. Not I, but it certainly tested my skill and ability during my first trip. While I've figured out the secret of success, and my son, Myles, and I cleaned the table during my second trip, technically speaking, the Tree River remains one of the most difficult of all rivers in the North Country to fish because it is so swift and turbulent in so many places.

On the northern edge of Canada's barren grounds lies the fly fisherman's Holy Grail—Nunavut's storied Tree River. Once smitten by it, a fly fisherman finds it almost impossible not to return for yet another tryst. It is a river like no other in Canada, home to the world-record Arctic char, a 32-pound, 9-ounce fish caught by Jeffery Ward on July 30, 1981. The river is so inaccessible and remote that absence really does make the heart grow fonder. It was only fitting that I returned with my son, Myles, in August, 2011, in search of what is akin to a Nirvana for many anglers—catching an Arctic char on a fly rod. Heck, never mind the challenge of catching one on a fly rod, I know some very good anglers who've been foiled on the Tree River fishing with hardware.

This trip was to be quite different from my first encounter with the Tree River a few years earlier in 2008 with David Webb, then-editor of the *Outdoor Edge* and *Western Sportsman* magazines, when we were truly humbled by the challenge to catch Arctic char on a fly rod. Yes, we both caught some fine char and lake trout; however, there were moments when things got a bit hairy, but that's another story.

Fishing the Tree River is no cakewalk!

The Tree River is in Canada's far north in the remote barren grounds, and Plummer's Arctic Lodges Tree River Lodge is undoubtedly one of the most remote fishing lodges in the country. Guests who take an excursion there from Plummer's Arctic Lodges Great Bear Lake Lodge fly some 373 km (232 mi) to the northeast over the desolate barrens, where the verdant Tree River valley stands out as an oasis.

Plummer's Arctic Lodges, Tree River Lodge.

Myles and I decided on a different approach compared with the one that David Webb and I took last time around. This time, we decided to focus on a four-day package on the Tree River that's a relatively new option in Plummer's Arctic Lodges excursions (www.plummerslodges.com) introduced a couple of years ago (they're now offering exclusive three-, four-, and seven-day Tree River Lodge packages not tied to trips to their main lodge on Great Bear Lake (www.plummerslodges.com/lodges/tree-river) in the NWT).

TREE RIVER RE-DO

Plummer's runs the Tree River Lodge as a satellite camp from Great Bear Lake, a fishermen's paradise. Rather than take a fly-out for a two-day trip to the Tree River from Bear (which David and I took the prior trip), Myles and I decided to first fly to Kugluktuk, Nunavut, then take a charter to the Tree River Lodge. We'd have to forego the fantastic lake trout fishing on Great Bear Lake and fly-outs for Arctic grayling on the Sulky River, but as the saying goes, you can't always have your cake and eat it too. This trip was all about fly fishing for Arctic char on the Tree River; forget everything else. Mind you there's nothing stopping you from spin fishing or jigging, both of which have many advantages over fly fishing in certain sections of the Tree, where decent casts with a fly rod are tough to make.

GUIDE ADVICE

Guides tend to favour either unobtrusive fly patterns for char, such as the Blue and Pink Rat wet flies, or the gaudy Pixie's Revenge. Other options are natural patterns that imitate sculpins. Plummer's guide Craig Blackie advised, "As in other systems, fresh fish are easy to catch, while fish that have been in the river awhile can become more difficult. Part of the issue relates to the conditions of the river. Early season sees the river high with snow melt and by August, the river is typically low and clear. That being said, a good rain can blow out the river at any time of year. What this means is that you must adjust your flies and tactics accordingly." Craig added: "A general rule of thumb is 8–10 wt. rods with heavy 12–15 ft. sink tips and large streamers or Spey flies. Productive patterns include Zonkers, Clouser Minnows, Lefty's Deceivers, Mickey Finns, and Spey flies, such as GPs and Popsicles. This approach applies when the fish are active; when they're not, use smaller, less obtrusive patterns fished with a strike indicator."

Getting to Kugluktuk was fairly straightforward. We took a flight on Canadian North from Edmonton to Yellowknife and then on to "Kug"—to use the local parlance for this Inuit settlement on the coast of the Arctic Ocean—which formerly went by the name of Coppermine. From Kug we boarded a Plummer's charter Turbo Otter floatplane for the last leg of our flight into the Tree River, a distance of about 130 km (80 mi) to the east. You can't help but feel just a little bit spooked when you're flying over Canada's barren lands near the Northwest Passage. The treeless, sweeping landscape has an ominous appearance haunted by the ghost of John Franklin, the English explorer whose mission to find the Northwest Passage failed when all 128 souls, including Franklin, were lost in 1845.

The day of our flight to the Tree River just happened to follow on the heels of a bona fide Arctic gale that had grounded the charter on Great Bear Lake due to poor flying weather. It's not uncommon for severe weather fronts stretching for hundreds of miles to blow inland from the Arctic Ocean in late August, and we bore witness to just such a storm, having to stay overnight at the Coppermine Inn in Kug (we got the last room in town—fortunately—happy to have a roof over our heads). Simply getting to your final destination is a bit of a challenge at times, which is yet another dimension of fishing in Canada's high Arctic.

TREE RIVER ANGLING

When we arrived at the Tree River, I felt like a kid at Disneyland. I couldn't believe it! Myles and I had the river to ourselves on day one of our trip and were actually the only people in the world who fished that day on the Tree River. *Wow!* The next day only three guests flew in from Great Bear Lake, so it was hardly what you'd call crowded.

After lunch we suited up and headed out for the afternoon bite with our fishing guide, camp manager Brad Eliason, who hails from Lake Louise, Alberta. Winds were out of the north and a light rain was falling with fog in the air. *Soucie's Field Guide of Fishing Facts* lists the preferred water temperature for Arctic char at 11–16°C (53–61°F), so when I checked the water temperature and found it was 10°C—where it would remain during our stay—I knew it would be perfect.

Third Falls on the Tree River, Nunavut.

It wasn't long before Myles joined the Arctic char club with a large char taken at the Montreal pool, named after a guide from this city. Naturally, celebrations were in order; your first Arctic char is a rite of passage in the fly-fishing fraternity. Fishing got better and better as our trip progressed for both char and lake trout until (sadly) we were told we had to leave to catch our plane back to Kug. We definitely broke through some fly-fishing barriers on the Tree River during our trip with numerous hook-ups and fish landed, many that taped 36 inches. It's all about being prepared, having the right tackle along with a good selection of fly patterns, and fishing strategically.

Myles Radford and one of many fine char caught on the Tree River.

We also experienced some novel twists in this trip from a culinary perspective. In addition to once again enjoying mouth-watering Arctic char sashimi, we feasted on tasty musk oxen steaks one evening. Taken by a hunter from the Great Bear Lake Lodge who generously shared some of his bounty, the musk ox was served with a delectable salad of wild (lemon) sorrel—a northern delicacy—with green peas and peppercorn. What a treat!

My advice to the itinerant angler who ventures to the Tree River is that while you don't have to be an Olympic athlete, you should be in good physical shape because walk-and-wade fishing on the barrens is no picnic. Plus, the Tree River riparian area is a veritable obstacle course in places, especially the east bank upstream of the lodge, which features slippery trails, a lot of uneven and rough cobble (that can be treacherous when wet), and generally tough slogging, particularly when the weather is poor. On the west bank there's a lot of spongy muskeg, so a trekking pole is an asset. A misstep can be fatal in places because the Tree River is a turbulent, dynamic river; with many rapids, falls, and spirited runs, it's impossible to ford. It's no surprise, then, that the Inuit name for the Tree River is *Kugluktoaluk*, which means "moving water" or "rushing waters." The Inuit had it right!

In sum, the fly-fishing drill on the Tree River is based on perseverance and optimism. Arctic char that have been in the river for a while can suffer from a case of lockjaw and are tough to catch; fresh fish are more cooperative. While you can often see the char, it's impossible to tell which kind of fish you're onto. With this in mind, cast into promising holding water using a classic "across and down" cast, mend your line, and fish the streamer in a dead drift. Naturally, you should also sight cast towards rising fish. After a couple of casts, take a few steps downstream and repeat the process. If you feel any kind of resistance, raise the tip of your fly rod and set the hook. Often, you may think you've got a snag because their bite is so hard, so if you get a hook-up, bring the fish to reel as soon as it's under control. Try to keep it out of fast water; otherwise, it might roll and likely throw the hook as barbless hooks are mandatory and are easily thrown.

As a last note, try not to miss the chance to hike to the upper falls on the Tree River—which is a barrier to upstream movement of char—a truly magnificent area in Canada's barrens to take pictures with the falls in the background.

Myles (L) & Duane Radford by the Third Falls on the Tree River.

B & J FLY FISHING ADVENTURES, EKALUK RIVER CHAR

by **Duane S. Radford**

> B & J Fly Fishing Adventures lodge manager Jack Elofsson is convinced that if anybody breaks the world record for Arctic char from the storied Tree River in Nunavut, it will be on the Ekaluk River on Victoria Island, high in the Canadian Archipelago—and Jack has the records to support his claim, so watch out. The Ekaluk River is a fly fisherman's joy, and B & J Fly Fishing Adventures only caters to fly fishers who will be put to the ultimate challenge to set a new record on this mighty river that flows into Wellington Bay on the Arctic Ocean.

B& J Fly Fishing Adventures is named after Bill and Jessie Lyall from Cambridge Bay, Nunavut, both of whom are Inuit. They've created a unique wilderness camp on the banks of the Ekaluk River on Victoria Island, which they've been operating in partnership with Jack Elofsson since 2001 during two-week periods (annually) in late August, at the peak of one of Canada's largest runs of Arctic char. Bill's quite the character—a natural-born leader and former member of the Legislative Assembly for the NWT territorial government, he was made a member of the Order of Canada in 2003 in recognition of his work with the Arctic Cooperative.

A former Swedish merchant mariner, Jack hails from Calgary, Alberta, and met Bill in 1984 when the Swedish *Lindblad Explorer* sailed through the Northwest Passage, the first passenger ship to complete the passage. Jack was a radio operator on the *Lindblad Explorer*, and Bill was mayor of Cambridge Bay at the time.

During my trip, Bill's son, Willy, helped out as a cook and camp attendant, along with Mike Mailey from Calgary, who works for SouthBow Fly & Tackle Ltd. Although Jack and Mike are both fly-fishing guides and provide advice and assistance if necessary, this is not a guided fish camp. You're expected to look after yourself.

Ekaluk River on Victoria Island, Nunavut.

As Jack isn't one to suffer fools gladly, B & J Fly Fishing Adventures caters to fly fishermen only—because they don't always get along well with gear fishermen on the same water. There's a level playing field on the Ekaluk River that only sees a handful of char fishermen at the camp each year; when I first looked into a booking, there was at least a two-year waiting list.

The "road" to Cambridge Bay goes through Edmonton for clients interested in an excursion on the Ekaluk River. Canadian North and First Air both fly into Cambridge Bay, with a stopover in Yellowknife. I flew with First Air, leaving Edmonton at 7:30 a.m. and fishing on the Ekaluk River in the early afternoon the same day.

Once I landed in Cambridge Bay, Bill Lyall's daughter, Fiona, picked me up at the airport and drove me to the floatplane dock on the Arctic Ocean. I was surprised that there were only two planes (an always reliable Beaver and a Cessna) that were operating out of Cambridge Bay—both owned by Fred Hamilton, who operates High Arctic Lodge—and both were in the air virtually nonstop during August, ferrying anglers in search of char, musk ox hunters, canoeists, etc.

FISHING NORTHERN CANADA *for* LAKE TROUT, GRAYLING *and* ARCTIC CHAR

If you're seeking a luxury getaway, you won't find it at B & J Fly Fishing Adventures camp; you won't be spending any time in a hot tub or sauna or sipping fine French Chardonnay with your dinner. Both Bill and Jack will tell you flat out that this is a wilderness camp, so you should be prepared for rustic, but comfortable, accommodations and home-cooked meals.

Willy Lyall with a plate of Arctic char sashimi.

Their goal is to provide you with a unique northern experience when it comes to cuisine. I feasted on char sashimi and chowder, baked char, Cajun char, roast musk ox, roasted caribou loin, and bannock—truly Arctic cuisine. Other meals feature what your body needs most during the trip—calories—because you'll be doing a lot of walk-and-wade fishing, day after day, until you board the floatplane for your return trip to Cam Bay.

I was in bed at 9:00 p.m. and up at 6:00 a.m. daily. It's all rather rigorous and it pays to get in shape before your trip; it's not a place for sissies, plus the weather can be foul at times, with gale-force winds.

Jack provided a "suggested equipment list," and it's vital to pack the equipment he recommends. If you forget something, don't expect them to have it in camp, which is about 70 km (45 mi) northwest of Cam Bay. And don't forget to pack at least one or two *spare* fly rods. I packed three 8-weight rods and broke my best and most expensive fly rod (in four places) on day two of my trip, something that's never happened to me before, just after I landed a 34-inch char (I had a tape so my measurements were accurate). I'd also suggest you bring spare fly line and backing because it's quite possible that a large char could run off with both.

Expect to see some musk ox during your trip and keep your eyes peeled for barren-ground grizzly bears, which crossed over to Victoria Island from the mainland on sea ice about 25 years ago. When I arrived Bill said there was a resident sow with two cubs a few miles outside of camp, but that

Jack Elofsson fillets an Arctic char beside the Ekaluk River.

they wouldn't likely venture near the Ekaluk River. To my surprise, I found fresh tracks of a grizzly bear the next day a few miles from camp. For this reason, I'd suggest you take bear spray and bear bangers (which I did pack), because I believe in always taking precautions when in bear country. I never did see the bear that made the tracks, which is a good thing, because there's no such thing as a tree on the tundra.

While there are no polar bears in the area to worry about, Bill cautioned us to stay clear of any musk ox because the rut had just ended, and bulls tend to be ornery post rut. As for other local animals, I did spot several during my stay, including an Arctic fox, a musk ox, golden eagles, lemmings, Canada geese, Jaegers, Herring gulls, and LBBs (little brown birds—sparrows).

IF YOU GO: Check out B & J Fly Fishing Adventures website: www.arcticflyfishing.com and Nunavut Tourism: www.nunavuttourism.com for trip-planning purposes.

I've done a lot of research on char waters in Canada's western arctic, and the only places that offer such opportunities are B & J

Fly Fishing Adventures and High Arctic Lodge (both on Victoria Island) in addition to Plummer's Arctic Lodges' Tree River Lodge. Plummer's will on occasion do fly-out trips to the Coppermine River from the main camp on Great Bear Lake, depending on water levels in the river, and as a side note, the stars lined up in my favour in August 2012—there was an opening at this exclusive char fishery due to some last-minute cancellations, and I was able to share the river with only five other guests. Although there were nine bookings for the second and last week at the camp, it wasn't exactly crowded!

The author with a fine Ekaluk River Arctic char.

I've fly-fished for all of Canada's salmonids and can say unequivocally that fresh char are near the top of the list in terms of the challenge in landing one with a fly rod. They have tremendous acceleration and can strip 100–200 feet of line in mere seconds; they're virtually unstoppable when they run downstream. If you don't chase them, they're gone! Char that have been in fresh water a while (after coming inland from the ocean to spawn) do not have nearly the same vigor.

You'll see lots of char in quiet water near the bank of the Ekaluk River and can sight cast to them, but they're wary, and if they spot you they'll dart into deeper, swift water (this is an avoidance response resulting from a long history of Inuit spearing char, definitely up to the '50s). Deceivers, Zonkers, and Woolly Bugger patterns will all take char, with pink probably being the most popular colour. Go-to flies can be obtained in the camp, and I'd have to say that the char fishing was outstanding. My largest fish taped 36 inches, and while I had to work for my char, on a good day my catches were in the double digits, almost unheard of in other riverine camps. The final verdict: the Ekaluk River is fully deserving of its reputation as one of the world's top char fisheries!

NUELTIN JOURNAL

by **C. Perry Munro**

> C. Perry Munro is an outdoor writer and artist who's a former Eastern Director of the Outdoor Writers of Canada. Perry lives on acreage near Wolfville, Nova Scotia, and is certified as a Nova Scotia Master Guide. Perry represents Nova Scotia on the National Recreational Fishing Awards Committee, and his travels have taken him to far-off destinations, including Labrador, Ungava, many saltwater fly-fishing destinations in the Caribbean, and in this article, Nueltin Lake on the border between Manitoba and Nunavut. Nueltin Lake is billed as "Canada's Original Catch & Release Lake" and enjoys a tradition of outstanding fishing for trophy lake trout. But, as Perry Munro writes and illustrates with his sketches, an Arctic adventure is about more than just a fishing trip.

Years ago my wife Judi was asked if she fished, to which she replied, "No, I don't, but I love where fish live!" The more I travelled to far-off fishing destinations, the more I saw the truth in what Judi had said. As a young man, the questions "How many?" "How big?" "Which species is the fish?" and "What do I use for tackle?" were my focus, but as the years passed, I became more attuned to the beauty and how things were connected wherever I fished. As a result, I started to carry a sketchpad and watercolour supplies along with my fishing tackle so I could sketch and reflect on what was important and of interest in my surroundings. These subsequently became an integral part of my journal.

When I was asked to join a group of anglers travelling to Nueltin Lake in northern Manitoba to fish for lake trout, northern pike, and grayling, I decided to keep a journal to record my sketches and thoughts while on the journey. I hope I have been able to convey the feelings and simple pleasures in the following segments that will enable you to see through my eyes the beauty in this remote and wonderful place.

KILLDEER'S NEST

We approach the shore for lunch and are greeted by a small bird with what appears to be a broken wing. It flutters and flops down the beach, hoping upon hope we will follow her away from the nest. We give pause as we also have an entourage of gulls following us and retreat to another area to start the fire. Before we give space to the killdeer, Jack, my fishing partner, sees the small nest and we marvel at it in the beach stones, amazed by the survival of a species that uses this remote beach on Nueltin Lake to hatch its eggs and raise its young. It's divine in its perfection.

UNINVITED GUESTS

We round a point and there are the seagulls. It's amazing that I haven't seen one all morning, yet there they are waiting for us to arrive for shore lunch. I don't have to look at my watch to see that it is 11:30 a.m. It's the same every day; uninvited guests swoop in to share our meal. I amuse myself by imagining I am critical to their survival, but looking around at the size and scope of my surroundings, I realize I am but a small contributor to these birds' dietary needs. Nonetheless, it's satisfying to feel you're needed.

STORMY WEATHER

The boat seemed big yesterday when we tried to get it through shallow water into a pike cove, but today it seems small. The waves pound the bottom and the vibration penetrates my spine. The fishing will be great when we get to sheltered water, and this will be but a memory of a great adventure.

SHORE LUNCH

The traditional shore lunch has numerous elements that makes this break in the middle of a fishing day memorable and important: the catching of a fish; the building of a fire; the preparation of the meal; the smells, tastes, and quiet conversations, all leading to a  satisfaction that often recalls another time—one when the catching and eating of fish was a necessity.

I have never had a shore lunch in a place that wasn't spectacular in its setting. The acquisition of game for the table is primal and gives a person an inner satisfaction. We at times are disconnected from the source of our food, and the shore lunch reacquaints us with that reality.

SKY AND WATER

 I was asked upon my return from Nueltin Lake what it was like, and my immediate response was that it featured seemingly endless sky and expansive water. Land was at times merely a line on the horizon, and you realize when you look across the water at the next landfall that this is a freshwater ocean, so to speak. As weather patterns form in the distance, you can sit in the sun and watch it rain miles away. As you do, you can't help but wonder why you always seem to be going towards the rain.

PIKE WATER

Whenever I approach pike water, I'm filled with anticipation because on Nueltin Lake, shallow coves lead off the main lake and you can just feel that pike are there. A pike's attraction to me is the unique and savage strike. He swims towards your fly, then a slight pause and a lightning strike with an explosion of water stops the heart and propels you to action. If they're in the thick weeds, you go in and chase them out to open water. There you have sight-fishing opportunities for cruising fish and watching giant pike turn towards your offering, where they engulf it in full sight as a memory not soon forgotten.

LAND OF THE MIDNIGHT SUN

Even during the darkest time of the night, there was enough light that I could still read a newspaper. I found that after dinner I had time to explore the area around the lodge, and the first place I wanted to explore was a river that entered into the lake about a mile away. The outfitter gave me permission to take a boat there in the evening to fish for grayling, so I tied the boat to a tree and proceeded up the river to find a place that was suitable for fly fishing. I'd started to fish and was releasing a grayling when I had a feeling I was being watched. I looked over my shoulder and saw a white wolf standing nearby, his eyes fixed on me. I slowly reached for my camera, but when I looked back, the wolf was no longer there. Sometimes you're in the right place at the right time, and although it didn't last long, this was one of those moments. In the morning I told my native guide of my encounter, and he informed me that I was one of few lucky enough to have had such an experience.

AT THE JOURNEY'S END

It is impossible not to admire the people who build, manage, and maintain the wilderness lodge accommodations. These individuals provide the opportunity for anglers to visit these wonderful places; without them, the Arctic—for ordinary people who wish to fish in extraordinary surroundings—would be an impossible place to travel and stay in such comfort and safety. To them we offer a debt of gratitude.

THE TRUE GEMS OF THE COPPERMINE RIVER

by **Faruk Ekich**

> The Coppermine River holds a unique place in the history of Canada for all the wrong reasons. It was at Bloody Falls on the Coppermine River that a band of Chipewyan and "Copper Indian" Dené, led by Samuel Hearne's guide and companion Matonabbee, massacred a camp of about 20 Inuit men, women, and children on July 17, 1771. The infamous incident occurred during Hearne's exploration of the Coppermine River, which has its origin at Lac de Gras, a small lake near Great Slave Lake, and flows generally north to Coronation Gulf where it empties into the Arctic Ocean at Kugluktuk (formerly known as Coppermine). Faruk Ekich lives in Ottawa, Ontario, and is the owner of Fly-tying Enhancements. This article describes his romantic adventures on the storied Coppermine River and his passion for Arctic char fishing.

Looking back at my lifelong passion—fly fishing—I consider myself very lucky. Not in terms of the number of fish and their size (the days of those values are over for me), but lucky to have lived in the places that provided me with the best opportunities to pursue my passion with all species of the Salmonidae family.

I grew up on the banks of the Vrbas, a beautiful limestone river that adorns the two-millennia-old town of Banja Luka in Bosnia. Like all of the rivers of that limestone region, the Vrbas is rich with aquatic life in which grayling, brown trout, and huge hutchen (landlocked salmon) were abundant. It is in that region that the first fly fishing was recorded by a passing Roman traveller in the third century.

It was practiced that same old way when I started to fish, just after WWII: lines braided from horse tail hair—terminating in a single hair for a tippet—limber hazelnut rods, and flies hand-tied at the river's edge, all to entice the "prince": grayling.

Bloody Falls on the Coppermine River.

Coming to Canada in 1966 was the most fortunate event for me. Apart from giving me the chance to establish a good life, it gave me the opportunity to expand my fly-fishing passion with Salmonids. My wife Ghislaine and I settled in Smithers, B.C.—a dream place for any steel-head fisherman —and the late sixties was a boom time to fish for that acrobat of the West. Later on, in 1970, we moved east and I waded, chest deep, in the Atlantic salmon paradise of Quebec.

The passion for salmon grabbed me so hard that I counted the rest of my life in terms of my ability to meet the king of our rivers on his terms. But as much as the grandeur and power of the salmon had a hold on me, I was charmed and gave my heart to the "princess" of the same waters—brook trout, otherwise known as *Salvelinus fontinalis*, the beautiful gem of the Salmonid family. It became a love affair that slowly took over. I went looking for it, in the best places where it lives, from James Bay to Hudson Bay to Ungava Bay, where I met the patriarch of Salvelinus, the Arctic char. Besides the power of salmon (many believe that char is the strongest salmonid), it has the beauty of *S. fontinalis* as well as a mysterious wildness about it. The surroundings in which it lives are majestic and challenging. Intrigued, I tried to find information on it, but apart from a few fishing adventure stories that offered very little or no information concerning fly fishing, I found only scattered scientific material like "The Arctic Char, Salvelinus Alpinus" by biologist Lionel Johnson, 1980.

In 1988 I contacted and met with the Johansons of Arctic Waterways, an outfit that used to run raft trips in the Canadian western Arctic. Fishing for Arctic char was one of the features they advertised as included in the trip on the Coppermine River. In reality, it was mainly a float trip down the river with the occasional opportunity to fish in the evenings, which did not suit my idea of a fishing trip.

I was already equipped with inflatable boats and other necessary gear for my fly-in trips to the Sutton River's seagoing brook trout on the west coast of Hudson Bay, so I decided to do it on my own and learn. From 1990 to 2004, I spent 15 Arctic summers fishing for anadromous char, all but one on the Coppermine River. The timing of the trips was generally from the second week in July, when the river sheds its ice, through the second week in August, before the cold weather sets in.

The Coppermine River flows 850 km (528 mi) from northeast of Yellowknife, NWT, to the Coronation Gulf in the Arctic Ocean. After my exploratory trip in 1990, which I started some 200 km (124 mi) from the sea, I established "my camp" at the junction of Melville Creek, located approximately 120 km (74 mi) by river upstream from the sea and the village of Kugluktuk (formerly known as Coppermine).

That section of the river is some 200–300 m wide, with an average depth of 1–2 m and a velocity of 6–7 km/hr. The banks are composed of about 20 m of high-boulder rubble, witness to the might of the ice force during the breakup. It is like that for another 15 km (9 mi) downstream, and then the river goes through the shale canyons for most of the way to the sea.

It is a unique river as it generates its own microclimate, allowing the tree line to extend into the tundra well above the Arctic Circle. The black spruce clings to wind-sheltered slopes of the valley through which the river flows, formed by the Coppermine and September Mountains, sculptured to perfect form by glacial artists. I wish I were able to describe the beauty it left there.

There is a rich history to it as well. Highly important to our First Nations people—both Dené and Inuit—as a source of pure copper, which shaped their culture, it was also used as a route to the Arctic Ocean by explorers such as Samuel Hearne, Sir John Franklin, and others. In the early

Faruk's camp at the junction of the Coppermine River and Mellville Creek.

'90s, this immense watershed was upset by the world's biggest discovery of diamonds. But to me, the real gem of the Coppermine River is its pristine wilderness of indescribable beauty that is home to barren-ground grizzly, musk oxen, caribou, and of course, the Arctic char and grayling.

From what I could understand in the scientific studies done in the lands of the Polar Basin from Siberia to Canada, Arctic char are anadromous freshwater fish that winter in lakes. Lionel Johnson writes in his work on char: "… melting snow caused by continuous sunshine of May and June, augments the flow, under the ice, of rivers that flow continuously throughout the winter, or causes flow to begin again where the river ice is solid. At this time anadromous Arctic char leave the still-frozen lakes and start their migration seaward. Simultaneously, the sea ice begins to melt and a lead develops between the land and the permanent pack ice. Within this lead there is considerable biological activity in spring, and it is upon the briefly abundant food resources developing here that anadromous char depend. After the relatively short period of intensive feeding, the Arctic char return to freshwater…"

The timing of return varies from region to region and year to year; the peak is generally in mid-August to early September. Lodges such as Plummer's Arctic Lodge on Great Bear Lake close after the first week of August due to the uncertainty of the weather, so it is wise to be well prepared if you stay past mid-August on your own. In the late eighties when I was researching char fishing, most believed that it would be very difficult, if not impossible, to get an anadromous char on the fly.

A fine char from the Coppermine River.

Knowing that similar beliefs were held about steelhead just 30 years before, I ignored them and used the same approach as steelhead fishermen did. That meant getting down to the fish with appropriate lines. The rod I used was a 9'6" fast-action Sage for 8-weight line. I used an anti-reverse reel, Hardy Ocean Prince, with a capacity approaching 400 yards in total. A second rod, a 6-weight Sage, was a compromise to be used for grayling and as a spare rod, while the lines were mainly shooting heads from 275 to 375 grain, sinking, with various densities. WF floating line, for dry fly fishing, was shortened at the back and a system of loop connections provided quick exchanges. I also carried my horse-hair line for traditional grayling fishing with hand-tied dry flies.

At first, the flies for char were a mixture of streamers and steelhead spays that imitated shrimp and minnows, tied on standard salmon hooks. They worked well enough, but there was a disadvantage to them that encouraged me to diversify from the traditional, hook-mounted fly. Here is an excerpt from a previous article I had written about it:

> Staying for three weeks at a time in the land of midnight sun with daylight around the clock, one spends lots of time fishing —sometimes as long as 16 hours per day. With the abundance of feeding fish, anyone can land an embarrassing number of fish there. The only challenge is how to release them in the best shape possible. Using the strong and heavy leader helped in shortening the exhausting fights and quicker releases. But, the *Salvelinus* family has a problem with coagulation, and the least amount of bleeding can result in a fish's fatality.

In my opinion, the traditional fly, with its long shank hook, has two major disadvantages for fish safety: the long shank and the point-down keeling. In the prolonged fight, the leaver of the long shank makes a larger hole (bigger wound), and the hook point down often gets the tongue hold where the blood vessels are.

There is a third disadvantage that may be of detriment for fish safety: in the pool that has been disturbed with a previous fight, fish lie low, and often in an attempt to get down to them, one snags a fish's back. The ensuing fight exhausts the fish (as well as the fisher trying to recover it for the release).

Step by step, I developed this concept of the Tube-Up fly with the fixed short shank hook held point up. In addition to reducing fish injuries, it offers the following advantages:

- Better holding than the long shank hook due to its shorter leaver
- Better hook-ups, especially on the downstream, hanging fly when the fish dives straight down after the rise. Closing its mouth on the fly at that downward position, the full width of the upper jaw is at the hook's point reach, rather than just a possible tip of the lower jaw when using the standard, point-down fly
- Reduces the frustrations of scrapped fly due to broken hooks
- Enables you to choose the much lighter hook for the desired gape on the large dry fly, which allows you to have a sparsely dressed fly with better floatability
- Hook gets disengaged from the fly at the beginning of the fight and fly stays out of harm's way of the fish teeth
- Tube Up, like the "keel fly," minimizes bottom snagging

This concept proved itself through several seasons, and I hope it can be of interest to you, especially char fishers. You can get instructions on how to tie them on my website:

www.ekichbobbin.com

CHAPTER 5 | NUNAVUT

Faruk Ekich with a Coppermine River char.

The final leg of the trip to my camp on the river is a 600-km (372-mile) flight from Yellowknife by floatplane. With a limit on weight and space, each item of gear has to be well chosen and minimized to support the needs of two over a three-week journey. Trips of this nature, unsupported, have to be well planned to be safe and enjoyable. Most important for me was the right partner. All eight people with whom I shared these trips were great companions, but two stand out: the late Serge Potvin from Lac St-Jean, and my friend and companion of seven trips, Bill Blatch, the "Franglais" from Bordeaux, France. As a well-known wine merchant and long-time Arctic traveller, he enhanced the trips with his hands-on teaching about that "civilized" drink. With the best vintages from Chateau Latour to Cheval Blanc, we crowned each stay there. As he put it: "We are now part of it all!"

There are great memories of hiking through untouched wilderness and encounters with all of its inhabitants—from sic-sic (ground squirrels), our camp landlords, and grizzlies to caribou, musk oxen, and wolves. But the most memorable are our snorkeling dives to dance with the char.

I kept a journal each day throughout these trips. The last day's entry, July 31, 2004, on the Escape Rapids, reads:

> *Now, at 21:45 we are sitting at our place on the ledge that offers a view of the rapids. East side of canyon is lit by mellow rays of the evening sun showing all of its many colours: dark gray basalt, whitewash streaks of some minerals brought down with seeping*

water, and rusty orange of lichens. We ate gurabija, the sweets that my mother prepared for each trip, and sipped on Armagnac. This is most likely my last time that I will sit here, so I am trying to memorize everything—from the smell of tundra flowers to the sound of rapids, chirping of swallows feeding their young just beside us, and the fall of "Sophy's Creek" from a 200-foot ledge. Will it be possible to show this to my grandchildren, Adam and Sophie, and will it be the same pure wilderness?

Escape Rapids on the Coppermine River.

CHAPTER 6

ONTARIO

IS THE SUTTON RIVER THE WORLD'S BEST BROOK TROUT RIVER?

by Ken Bailey

Ken Bailey is an award-winning Canadian writer who is the Hunting Editor for *Outdoor Canada*, Canada's largest outdoor magazine. Ken lives in Edmonton, Alberta, where he's employed as the Managing Director of the Alberta Professional Outfitters Society. In this article he describes a float trip he and his buddy David (Dave) Kay made down the renowned Sutton River in northern Ontario. He's well travelled and if he queries whether the Sutton River is the world's best brook trout river, listen up. This is an article the co-editors just couldn't pass up for inclusion in this book about fishing in northern Canada because it features one of the world's premier brook trout fisheries.

It's well documented that anglers are, by nature, liars. Prevaricators might be the politically correct term if you're so inclined. No wonder, then, it was with jaundiced eyes that I read the revised 2002 edition of *Brook Trout,* or more specifically, the new chapter that author Nick Karas entitled "The World's Best Brook Trout River."

Really? *The* best brook trout river in the world? That's quite a bold statement, although I suppose not an unusual one for a fisherman, let alone a fisherman who is by vocation a storyteller. Still, the description of the river seemed to ring true, and Karas is, after all, widely regarded as—dare I say it?—one of the world's best and most knowledgeable brook trout anglers.

And so it was that I took more notice than I might have otherwise when I saw a promotion for fly-in trips to northern Ontario's Sutton River. Or should I say *the* Sutton, the very river Karas was describing in his new chapter when he complained, "Our biggest difficulty was finding small fish for the frying pan."

Right away I knew there was just one thing to do—see for myself if Karas' claims were true. And I knew in a flash whom I'd ask to come along. Dave Kay and I have shared more than a few angling and hunting adventures over the years, and the Sutton's remote wilderness setting would be right up his alley.

Getting to the Sutton is a logistical challenge. From my home in Edmonton, Alberta, it meant a flight to Toronto, Ontario, followed by another flight north to Timmins. There we bought groceries and stayed overnight in a local motel, then drove three hours farther north to the Town of Hearst. From there, it was another couple of hours by floatplane via Hearst Air to Hawley Lake, the Sutton's headwaters.

Tent camp on the Sutton River.

The Sutton is not a particularly challenging river to navigate once you get there—it's just a helluva long way from civilization. Sliding languidly into Hudson Bay on the west side of James Bay, it's a mere 130 km (80 mi) long, and most who paddle its length cover the distance in an easy 6–10 days, depending on how they want to spilt their time between paddling and fishing. Dave and I planned for nine days in all.

Albert Chookomoolin, a Cree born in 1949 in a mud hut at Hawley Lake, is the Sutton's unofficial river keeper. He still lives on the river with his wife and two sons, guiding anglers by way of a motorized canoe, taking them downstream a short distance to one of his tent camps where they overnight. Other than that, Albert's clients don't see much of the river. But then, they're there to catch fish and, as we were to learn, you can wear out your best rod and reel on big brook trout in the Sutton's first 15 or so kilometres (9 miles). Dave and I planned, instead, to see it all, paddling the entire river by ourselves. Albert stores canoes for Hearst Air, and after picking one out of the mix and carefully loading our tent, grub, fishing gear, and other necessities, we shoved off. After day two, when we passed Albert's tent camp, we wouldn't see another soul until we met our floatplane at Hudson Bay. Mission creep was not an option—once we were headed downstream, we had no choice but to make it to the pickup point on time.

On canoe trips the tendency is to make some miles the first day, loosening unused muscles and getting in sync with your paddling partner. But for Dave and me, an hour of cruising over pools teeming with colourful, fat brook trout was about an hour more than we could stand. So we soon stopped and began casting flies over likely looking runs.

In short order we'd each hooked and landed several brookies up to 21 inches long. Like anxious football players, anglers can't relax until they get that first hit out of the way, and this initial stop did the trick. We cast knowing smiles at one another—if this was going to be a harbinger of what lay ahead, the trip would definitely be one to remember.

Brook trout are the old souls of Canada's game fish. They just want to be left alone, and if they could, I'm sure they'd cuss at anglers, telling them to get the hell off their property. And unlike some of their trout and char brethren, brook trout aren't newcomer transplants from abroad, and most don't venture on sea cruises only to come back fat and lazy. No, brookies are working fish, doing what they've done in solitude for millennia, long before the first natives dangled a grasshopper on a bone hook in front of them. And lest we forget, they are arguably the most beautiful fish on our good earth.

Unfortunately, the distribution and average size of the species have diminished throughout most of its range because of development and fishing pressure. On the remote Sutton, however, brook trout can still reach their full potential in terms of numbers and size—and Dave and I aimed to take full advantage of that.

Over the days, we settled into an easy routine. We woke whenever we felt like it, brewed some fresh java over a fire, then waded lazily up and down the river as the mood struck us, casting as we went. If it's true that the greatest gift one fly fisherman can bestow upon another is to walk 100 m in the opposite direction, then it was Christmas most days on the Sutton. We both revelled in the solitude of a few hours alone on a pristine wild river, crammed with hefty, eager trout. Catching fish was never a problem, and we quickly gave up counting those brought to the net.

Sutton River brook and fly box.

Dave and I both enjoy the lore and legend described in historic brook trout literature, so we'd come well stocked with classic, glamorous brookie flies, determined to fish the river the traditional way. My fly wallet was crammed with time-tested Montreals, Trout Fins, Colonel Fullers and, of course, venerable Parmachene Belles. Well, I'm here to tell you that Sutton brook trout aren't the urban dandies of the Beaverkill River and similar streams in the Catskills and Adirondacks that have garnered so much press over the years—they wanted no part of anything dainty.

Despite making hundreds of casts, I managed to hook only one trout swinging my classic wet flies down and across. Talk about taking a knife to a gun fight. But every time I tied on a big streamer, a scrum of broad-shouldered squaretails chased it down like a greyhound after a mechanical rabbit. And, as it turned out, the bigger and rougher the fly, the better, with top choices including Bow River Buggers and Muddler Minnows. When the streamers wore out their welcome, skittering a chunky floating mouse pattern across the surface was sure to elicit a strike.

Around noon each day, we wandered back to camp, had a quick lunch, pulled up stakes, and paddled until mid-afternoon before choosing our next campsite. We'd then fish through the late afternoon and early evening, keeping a couple of trout for dinner. Dave is a cook of no insignificant talents, and every night he crafted meals befitting the grandest restaurants.

I knew my place and was quite content to handle cleanup chores, knowing full well I was reaping the better part of the deal. For when Dave wasn't baking teriyaki-style fillets or frying fish in a ponzu-onion sauce, he was picking wild berries and making his own black currant jam. We might have been sleeping on the ground floor, but thanks to Dave we were dining in the penthouse every night.

When you're paddling and fishing the days away, and sleeping in a tent every night, the weather takes on more significance than it would at home. Our first four days on the water saw clear blue skies, no wind, and a sweltering sun—perfect conditions for a wilderness fishing trip, some might suggest. But warm weather comes at a cost in these parts, with mosquitoes and blackflies emerging in droves and turning each day into a battle of physical and mental endurance. Fortunately the overcast and drizzly skies and cool air that greeted us through most of the latter half of the trip offered some welcome respite. As for the eager fish, well, they didn't seem to care one way or the other about the weather.

In many respects, the Sutton is an innocuous, if deceptive, river. In most places it's 60–100 metres wide and relatively flat. There's no whitewater to speak of, but the boulder gardens are numerous and late-season paddlers need to be wary of shallow sections. Though some pools could hide a semi-trailer, you can ford the river on foot across most of the runs. The banks are generally abrupt, and willows line much of the shoreline, placing decent camping spots at a premium. Miss one, and it can be several kilometres until the next suitable pull-out appears.

Shrouding the shoreline willows is a drunken array of spruce and tamarack, leading you to believe the river cuts through a vast tract of boreal forest. It's all smoke and mirrors, however, as the trees only extend back 100 metres or so before giving way to flat, relatively featureless tundra. The first time you hike from the river to the tundra, you quickly become aware that you're well into northern Canada, a startling reminder that creature comforts are a long, long way away. The fact that you're also paddling through Polar Bear Provincial Park is another clue you're deep in the wilderness, and the reason you're always within spitting distance of a shotgun and slugs.

As I reflect on our days on the Sutton, I suppose I should be telling you about bent rods and one big hard-fighting fish or another, or the sage old trout in a corner pool that took me eight different flies and two patient hours to fool. But the truth is, the fish were so plentiful and so darn big on average that the memory of one fades quickly into another. You simply can't separate one fish, one pool, or even one day from another. And yet despite the numbers of fish, you can't become jaded on the Sutton because the experience is simply too incredible. There are few dips and valleys —it's all one big high.

Ken with a Sutton River brook trout.

To be fair, neither Dave nor I landed one of the seven-pound bruisers that swim these waters, as evidenced by the photos I've seen and the stories I've heard from others. But we caught enough wild halos in the three- to five-pound range to last several lifetimes, and I don't believe we caught two fish shorter than 16 inches over the entire nine days. It was one of those adventures where you can only tell people, "You had to be there to believe it."

And as for Nick Karas? I can find no argument as to why the Sutton doesn't deserve his praise as the best brook trout river in the world.

SUTTON PRIMER: Still not convinced the Sutton is the world's best brook trout river? If you want to put the claim to the test yourself, here are a few tips to get you started.

GETTING THERE: Return charter services to the Sutton can be arranged through Hearst, Ontario's Hearst Air, which also provides canoes and leases satellite phones to ensure you can call for help in case of an emergency. If you prefer to be guided, Hearst Air will set you up with Albert Chookomoolin and his tent camps. Contact: 1-866-844-5700; www.hearstair.com.

GEAR: As with any fly-in canoe trip, you need to pack light. My Black Diamond Vista was the perfect tent choice for accommodating two big guys and all their gear. Quality rain gear is a must, as are bug jackets and insect repellent. Brook trout are unparalleled for eating, so don't worry about bringing meat along. Pack your food in airtight containers, as there are polar bears wandering the area.

TACKLE: Fly anglers should pack 6- to 8-weight rods. You'll get by with floating lines 90 percent of the time, but a sink tip is useful on some deeper pools. Bring along plenty of large streamers in brown, black, and orange; for top water action, mouse patterns and extra-large stimulators produced best. Breathable chest waders and a landing net are invaluable.

MORE INFO: The fine folks at the Sault Ste. Marie, Ontario-based Algoma Kinniwabi Travel Association can provide plenty of information and tips for travelling to the region. Contact: 1-800-263-2546; www.algomacountry.com.

CHAPTER 7

QUEBEC & LABRADOR

CONFESSIONS OF A GEORGE RIVER (QUEBEC) JUNKIE

by **Ken Bailey**

> The George River in northwestern Quebec is one of northern Canada's most storied Atlantic salmon streams, a large, often raging river in the Ungava wilderness like no other. Ken Bailey's fly-fishing abilities were tested to the limit during his trip on this river in search of legendary Atlantic salmon, which have likely broken more fishermen's hearts than any other fish in Canada, and for good reason—they're immensely powerful creatures of some of the wildest places on the planet. Fishing for them can—and often is—a truly humbling experience, and for many anglers all they'll ever recall is the thrill of a swirl as an Atlantic salmon rises towards their presentation, sans any hook-up, nothing more. This informative article is a must-read for Atlantic salmon fly-fishing aficionados or novices who want to challenge themselves in pursuit of one of Canada's most sought-after fish.

You can do everything absolutely right in a battle with an Atlantic salmon and still come out second best. While that may not seem particularly fair, it's this very uncertainty, the utter lack of assuredness every time you hook into one, that gives the Atlantic salmon its legendary status within angling circles.

Of course, it doesn't exactly boost your confidence, especially after it's already been knocked to the rocks a few times, to hear your guide chant, "Back to the kiddie pool for you!" And this after you've failed, yet again, to tame 15 pounds of raw, northern flesh and will. But I was prepared for that when I ventured to Helen's Falls Salmon Camp in northern Quebec's remote Ungava Peninsula in 2007.

After all, the invitation from outfitter Sammy Cantafio had come with its own special brand of admonishment—he made it clear he was going to teach me how to fish Atlantic salmon on the famed George River, but that I was going to have to be willing to listen and learn. These fish, he warned, have a way of unceremoniously dismissing the uninitiated or unskilled. His words were prophetic, as I was to soon discover.

Following a 20-minute boat ride upstream from camp on day one, we beached below Pool 1, the aptly named first of a dozen or so pools over one of the most gorgeous stretches of wilderness river you could ever hope to wade. For three kilometres, a series of ledges, falls, and chutes collectively form the first major obstacle for Atlantic salmon on their way upstream from the saltwater of the Hudson Strait to their spawning beds on the upper George.

Fly fishing on the George River.

Before turning me loose on the pool, Sammy gave me a series of instructions, beginning and ending with, "Wait until you actually see or feel a fish take your fly before you set the hook." About 10 minutes later, a silver form rose from the dark, deep water below my fly as it skittered across the current. I set the hook—before I saw or felt the fish take my fly.

There it was, lesson number one, shot to hell already. I groaned at my rookie mistake. Sammy just shook his head in equal parts amusement and feigned disgust, and I went back to casting. Three hours of instruction, repeated casting, and no fish later, it was time to head back to camp for supper.

After dinner, Sammy and I talked fishing until the wee hours. There was only one other serious angler in camp—Rick Yeiser, a teacher from Vermont who was enjoying his 24th consecutive year fishing the George—but he'd hit the hay early. So over a couple of hours and a couple of sundowners, Sammy talked about his life in the North, of Atlantic salmon, and of his passion for fishing, all the while imparting little nuggets of information that would turn out to be of immense value in the coming days on the water.

I'd first met Sammy a few years earlier when he invited me up for an Ungava caribou hunt. Over the week I spent in pursuit of big bulls, as well as world-class brook trout, I learned what many others had long before discovered—that Sammy's operations are top-drawer, from his camps and guides to the game and fish populations that inhabit this area in Quebec's northernmost extremes.

A lifelong hunting and fishing addict, Sammy started his career in sales, a vocation that serves him well to this day. He has that unique way of making you feel good, even when he's dressing you down, as I learned firsthand every time another silvery beauty escaped back into its pool. A yearning for adventure soon led him down a different career path, however, and he qualified first as a private pilot, then as a commercial pilot and instructor.

Eventually tiring of flying full-time, Sammy followed his nose north and settled in Kuujjuaq, a small community on the Koksoak River just south of Ungava Bay. By then, all the ingredients were in place: a love of the outdoors, a pilot's licence, connections in the North, and a knack for salesmanship. And oh yeah, he's a professional fly tier to boot. Life as an outfitter was all but inevitable at that point, and Sammy has been living both the romance and the adversity of the profession for more than 25 years now.

The next morning after breakfast, Sammy introduced me to Nathan Wellman, a young man who would be my guide for the rest of my six-day stay. Sammy's angling advice must have sunk in during my hours of sleep, as I began the day with two salmon hooked, played, and landed before 9:00 a.m. Though neither was particularly large—one about eight pounds, the other a pound or so less—they were honest-to-God Atlantic salmon. And I was no longer a salmon virgin.

Over the years, I've read plenty on fly fishing for Atlantic salmon, and these fish performed as advertised, rising suddenly and spectacularly, stretching to the sky before throwing off soul-stirring plumes of water as they crashed back down.

The river was unusually high during my visit, adding an extra challenge. Some of the best pools disappear altogether in high water, and the salmon move through much more quickly than normal, unencumbered by the usual chicane of rocks and ledges. As a result, we skipped straight from Pool 2, where I'd landed the second fish, up to Pool 5½.

It was slow going. The George's shoreline reminded me of pictures I've seen of Mount Everest's base camp, with broad sheets of angled granite pocked by a veritable minefield of ankle-destroying boulders. And it was made all the more treacherous by a steady drizzle, causing the rocks to be much more slippery than usual.

When we arrived at Pool 5½, I hadn't made 10 downstream-and-across casts when the water around my #6 Green Monster erupted and I had another fish on. I was just beginning to figure I had this whole salmon game sussed when the fish, a beautiful 12-pounder, cleared the water, shook its head, and spit the hook at me in clear disdain.

I turned to Sammy, eyes lowered, waiting for what I knew was coming. "Lower your rod, and bow to the fish when it jumps, Ken," he scolded. "Remember what we talked about!" Although I'd had little previous Atlantic salmon experience—just two fishless days on the infamous Miramichi in New Brunswick—I'm no rookie angler. And since I know how to play a fish, I could only agree with Sammy's assessment and chastise myself accordingly for mistakes I knew better than to make.

As it turned out, the rest of the day was fishless; a few would follow, some would roll under the fly, and others would refuse at the very last second. As I was learning, this is typical behaviour for Atlantic salmon, fish as renowned for being picky about what they eat as high-paid supermodels.

The next morning greeted us with cool, nervous weather, the clouds clinging to the valley walls and dropping a steady mist of rain that was to not let up all day. Nathan, Sammy, and I jumped into our boat for the by now familiar short trip upstream. The George is a broad, brawling river, with a strong current that was only strengthening as the water continued to rise. It was now some four or five feet higher than the norm, and we were losing accessible pools by the day.

Despite the George's tumultuous personality, Nathan guided the boat upstream with the assurance of someone who's lived on the water his whole life. That wasn't surprising considering that he, like most of Sammy's guides, grew up in a small fishing community on the remote north shore of the St. Lawrence. Nathan's father is a lobsterman, and when Nathan isn't guiding, he's at home pulling traps, setting nets, and generally making his living out of a boat.

Sammy's guides are not the type you'll see gracing the cover of the Orvis catalogue, decked out in the latest fishing fashions. No, the standard guide's uniform at Helen's Falls consists of blue jeans, working shirts, rubber boots, and yellow rain slickers. But as I quickly discovered, what these guys may lose in style points, they more than make up for in hard work, know-how on the water, and a true passion for fishing. These are fellows with fish tattooed on their souls, the kind of guides you can only hope to get when you step out of a floatplane onto the shores of a remote lake or river. They all speak with what I would loosely describe as a Newfoundland accent, and although I couldn't always discern the specific words that Nathan was saying, I always knew exactly what he meant.

The morning's fishing treated me exactly as the weather did—with little sympathy. In the first two hours I hooked and subsequently lost three fish, including one that would have approached the 20-pound class, a true trophy salmon for this river. Unlike some of the more famous New Brunswick and Quebec rivers, where 30-pound-plus Atlantics are hooked every year, 25 pounds is about the largest you can expect on the George, with anything more than 15 considered a really nice fish.

The first two salmon broke my leader on rocks, while the third —the biggest—jumped across the pool then slid down a chute and over a ledge before I could react. When I did attempt to address the situation, I simply clamped down on my reel and, naturally, broke the leader. In hindsight, if I'd just let the fish go down to the pool below, I could have scrambled down the rocks and fought it from there. Another rookie mistake.

With every hooked and lost fish, Sammy and Nathan were only stepping up their good-natured jibes. "Back to the kiddie pool!" "My two-year-old could have landed that one!" "Back on the training wheels for you!" That last taunt was a reference to salmon flies with two hooks that help ensure you stay connected to a fish as it leaps and thrashes. After the previous day, my confidence had been soaring; now it was back on the rocks as I struggled to understand why I was having such dismal results. I was learning my salmon lessons, I guess, the only way one can—through trial and error, and heartbreak.

I was also starting to understand the addictive nature of Atlantic salmon angling. This is fishing with a purpose; every cast must be precise, every swing of the fly followed with clear-eyed intensity. And once you hook an Atlantic, you experience a feeling unlike anything else—a feeling that everything else in the world can, and should, be put on hold.

My biggest tactical error, I was beginning to realize, was that I was playing these fish, not fighting them. There's simply no room for the timid or lackadaisical here. You're battling a fish that is willful and game to the core, fighting as though it has absolutely nothing to lose.

Compounding what the fish themselves bring to the table, everything on the George takes place in relatively cramped quarters. The fish-holding lies are about the size of your dinner table, and the pool they're resting in is likely to be no bigger than your combined dining room and living room. You have to keep them in that pool, too, or they'll be gone forever. And don't let them swim around, or under, any of the refrigerator-sized boulders that litter the pool bottom, or they'll break off.

They'll also break off if you don't give them just the right amount of slack when they leap—and trust me, they all leap. If you don't turn their heads back when they start swimming away, they'll spit the hook. And even when you do it all right, there's still about a fifty-fifty chance they'll somehow escape. Truly wild creatures have instincts for survival that most of us will never understand.

It's because of all that, I was learning, that Atlantic salmon fishing is unlike any other fishing you'll experience.

In the world of Atlantic salmon, the George River is one of the most coveted destinations. Consider Rick Yeiser, the teacher from Vermont. He fishes three solid weeks every year: one week for brown trout in Argentina, another for steelhead on Alaska's Kodiak Island, and a week on the George for Atlantic salmon. He's fished virtually every famous Atlantic salmon river on the planet, but he's been coming back to the George for almost a quarter century. When I asked him why, he said there's simply no other river that consistently produces as many Atlantics under such exciting and challenging conditions. Coming from an angler with his credentials, I'd say there's no higher praise for a river.

While I was beginning to feel the stirrings of my own growing addiction, the fish were pretty much "owning" me, as my boys would describe it, not the other way around. Shore lunch provided a much-needed respite from my series of lost fish on that third morning, then it was back into the water at Pool 6. In no time I hooked and landed a fish—not a very big one, but it was just the confidence-booster I needed.

We then wandered back to Pool 5½, and I worked the water methodically for an hour with nothing to show for my efforts but a tired arm. "Two more casts, Ken," Nathan eventually hollered from shore. I edged out a little farther into the swirling water and cast again, with the lie I was trying to reach at the outer limits of my casting ability. Bingo! My fly disappeared in a swirl and I was into a salmon.

Feeling the resistance of my line, the fish surged skyward, revealing its broad flanks. This one would go 15 pounds for sure, I thought, and I made every effort to remember all I'd learned as the salmon tore back and forth across the pool. Every time it made a run for the life-saving turbulence of the main current, I leaned back on my rod until I was sure something—the rod, the line, or the fish—would break. And each time the salmon would give a little, then slash its way back to the pool's centre. Then it would invariably leap, and I'd bow to it; I was fighting this fish, not playing it. And I was winning. Twenty minutes after the battle started, Nathan slid the big net under the salmon.

Ken Bailey (R) landing an Atlantic salmon.

It was a great way to end the day, so we jubilantly headed back to Pool 1, where we had beached the boat earlier. Along the way we came to Pool 2, which had already defeated me that very morning. Nathan suggested we give it a quick try; supper could always wait a few minutes. So I tied on Sammy's favourite fly, a #8 Green Cross, and started to work the water.

Cast, swing, retrieve. Cast, swing, retrieve. It was on about my tenth cast that I saw a dark-backed salmon rise up under my fly and engulf it. As before, I patiently but firmly worked the fish, feeling more in control than I'd been yet. Eventually, it too succumbed, and as we motored back to camp and to the warmth and good food that awaited, I reflected on the highs and lows of my day: seven Atlantic salmon hooked, four landed. All in all, I wouldn't have wanted it to unfold any other way.

Ken Bailey with a George River Atlantic salmon.

The last couple of days in camp were a little more varied. I got to see more of the George, with Nathan and Sammy taking me to some of their favourite hotspots, and I fished for brookies and lakers. While I thoroughly enjoyed hooking them—especially the beautifully hued brook trout—I couldn't get my mind off the Atlantic salmon. Even a side trip up the Ford River, a tributary of the George, to see if the Arctic char run had started couldn't pry my thoughts from Helen's Falls, the pools, and the salmon.

My final day in camp allowed for only a few hours of fishing, but I was at least able to feed my new addiction by landing the only two salmon I hooked. Eventually, however, the Twin Otter touched down and there was little to say or do but shake hands, express my gratitude, and keep a stiff upper lip as I climbed aboard. As we pulled sharply off the gravel airstrip, I slouched back in my seat, reflecting on what I'd learned. Finally, I understood the allure of the Atlantic salmon.

And while the future of this wonderful fish across much of its home waters remains precarious, the George River had allowed me, if only for a few days, to gain a deeper understanding of the traditions and lore of salmon angling. More than anything, though, I discovered that this type of fishing is not for the mere lucky. It's for those who persevere, exhibit patience, and are willing to hone their skills to the highest level. It's for those who can finally and fully understand that when they go Atlantic salmon fishing, it's not really the fish they're after.

GETTING THERE: First Air runs daily flights from Montreal into Kuujjuaq. From there, Ungava area outfitters fly guests into their respective camps using charter air services. My trip to the George River and Helen's Falls was with Ungava Adventures, the only outfitter providing fishing services on the river.

ACCOMMODATIONS: I stayed at Helen's Falls Salmon Camp, run by Sammy Sammy's Ungava Adventures. The comfortable, heated cabins have hot running water, and on-site staff prepare wonderful homestyle meals, including fresh bread and pastries. Shore lunches are hearty and tasty. Don't go to camp expecting to lose weight.

WHEN TO GO: Helen's Falls Salmon Camp is open from mid-July to early September, with excellent fishing on offer throughout.

PERMITS: A Quebec fishing licence is required (Ungava Adventures includes the licence in its package).

GEAR: For Atlantic salmon, an 8- or 9-weight fly rod spooled with a weight-forward floating line is best. Quality reels with a smooth, reliable drag system are a must. An 8-weight rig is ideal for the area's lake trout and Arctic char; bring a sink-tip line as well as a floating line. For brook trout, a 6-weight rod with floating and sink-tip lines will cover all opportunities.

CLOTHING: Quality rainwear is a must, as is a warm wool or fleece jacket, and you'll need breathable chest waders to access the prime pools. The weather can be unpredictable, so bring a warm hat and gloves. Polarized sunglasses are a must. The camp provides a complete list of recommended clothing and gear; follow it and you won't go wrong.

MORE INFO: Ungava Adventures, 1-866-444-3445; www.ungava-adventures.com. Tourism Quebec, 1-877-266-5687.

FLOWERS RIVER LODGE (LABRADOR) CHANGEOVER

by C. Perry Munro

> The Flowers River Lodge is located in northern Labrador and boasts Atlantic salmon that top 30 pounds, as well as exciting Arctic char fishing later in the season. Atlantic salmon fishing is so good at this lodge that bookings sell out years in advance. Nova Scotia fishing guide Perry Munro is no stranger to Arctic fly-fishing adventures. In this article, he shares his love of the North Country at the Flowers River Lodge, Labrador, at the beginning and close of the season. The "changeover" is a nostalgic time at any lodge, as staff gear up for the start and end of the season.

I settle back in my seat in the de Havilland Beaver floatplane as we taxi out to depart for Flowers River Lodge in northern Labrador. As we prepare for takeoff at the close of the season, I reflect back to opening the lodge just two months prior, contemplating the activities at the lodge, the people who came to fish for salmon, and those who run the well-oiled machine that allows anglers to enjoy fishing in the wilds of northern Labrador in success, comfort, and safety.

My journeys to Flowers River Lodge started at the Dieppe Fly-Fishing Show in Moncton, New Brunswick, where I had a booth to display my artwork. Jim Burton, the outfitter-owner of Flowers River Lodge had a booth there as well, and he expressed an interest in having some carvings done on-site at the lodge. So, we made arrangements and in early July, I departed for Labrador. I spent a busy week carving and helping get the lodge ready for the arrival of anglers (at least I thought I was a help!).

There was an ice pack in the Labrador Sea, so unfortunately, the salmon didn't arrive during my stay—which made it the first time in all my visits to Labrador that I hadn't wet a line. Upon hearing this, Jim assured me that would be remedied if I would return the last week of the season (September 1–8, 2013). In my experience, a new river is always exciting because each one is unique, featuring a different character with similarities all to be explored and discovered. Having been a fishing guide for over four decades and fished and guided on a number of salmon rivers, seeing the beauty and potential of the Flowers River on my first trip made an upcoming one irresistible. *Game on!*

The plane was loaded at Otter Creek, the floatplane facility near Goose Bay, early in the morning my first day back in September. The anglers met and it looked like a great group—Dwight Blackwood; Joe McKinnon; Dan Locke, from *Newfoundland Sportsman* magazine; Cody Fitzpatrick, the winner of the contest sponsored by *Newfoundland Sportsman* and his dad, Dave; Chad Gosse; Lester Antle, a first-time salmon angler; and me. We departed for the Flowers River in anticipation of a great week of salmon fishing.

For the staff at the lodge, the arrival/departure of guests is always a major changeover. The fusion of the incoming guests with those departing represents a wonderful sharing of a common interest. Questions fly: "How did you do?" "What flies were hot?" and the departing answer the arrivals' questions with the satisfaction of sharing success.

Behind all the excitement and conversation among the clients, the staff is busy unloading the incoming baggage from the plane and loading departing baggage, like a well-rehearsed ballet. The kitchen gets restocked, the luggage is distributed to assigned rooms, and introductions are made. After that, the rush is on to get on the water and wet a line. *Changeover complete!*

My assigned guide was Ed Dominey—the inventor of the Bumble Bee fly, one I had never seen or used, but that was to change in a hurry. My fishing partner, Dan, was a member of the film crew, so when he was part of the shooting schedule, I had assigned pools to myself.

Whether alone or not, I knew to heed the best piece of advice I have received in my angling adventures: Listen to your guide! No matter how experienced you are on your home water and other rivers, your guide is an expert on his river and the go-to flies. Methods and techniques change from river to river, so it's important to pay attention; some guides offer advice, and if not taken or tried, they won't make the suggestion again. You can't go wrong taking your guide's advice to get you off to a good start.

The flies were quite simple but the size surprised me. We used Bumble Bee, Orange Bug, and Bombers in sizes 6, 8, and 10 for dry flies; Ed recommended the Undertaker, Black Bear Green Butt, and Blue Charm in sizes 8, 10 and 12 for wet flies, which were "riffle hitched" and worked well if presentation was perfected. This is where I initially had a problem. [Editor's note: The "Riffle Hitch" or "Riffling Hitch" is a knot that makes a fly skim across the surface of a river or stream to attract fish feeding near the surface. It's usually used by salmon and steelhead anglers; however, it can also be highly effective for trout.]

Usually when I cast a wet fly for salmon, I cast 45 degrees across the river and then throw an upstream mend in the line to get a good drift and presentation. When I started to do this with no success, Ed advised me to cast upstream without a mend. This formed a bag in my line when the water velocity was higher in the middle of the river, and the fly would speed up because of the bag. Ed kept asking me to cast higher until the cast was straight across until—bang! Fish on!

This was how it seemed to work—with some pools requiring a slightly different angle of presentation, as observed by the wake of the Riffled fly—and I came to believe the slow current required this technique to speed up the fly in the strike zone. Dry fly presentation, however, was easier as it was basically a dead drift, and to say this was perfect dry-fly water is an understatement. A low-gradient, slow-moving current with moderate depth makes the presentation easy to master.

Once I had the presentation down pat, I had success on different flies, but the best for me at this point was a Riffled Undertaker and a Bumble Bee, both size 10. The river was low and very clear, rivaling the Gaspe Rivers in Quebec in clarity, so one had to cast with care and not alarm the fish. That said, the longest cast would not be over 70 feet, with most short of that as the pools were well defined and provided in most cases open casting with no backcast problems. Each day you had a different assignment of pools to fish, and you were able to fish all available pools at least once. Everyone who had fished there before looked forward to fishing the "Top Pool," and so it was with anticipation that I looked forward to my turn at this famous spot. Tomorrow would be the big day!

To arrive at the Top Pool, we went upstream seven kilometres until we came to a series of rapids, then met the anglers who went up the day before and had another changeover. After exchanging the latest news, we started a portage that took us nearly two miles to the top of the rapids. We then travelled through woods, edges of bogs, and ridges before arriving at a wooded campsite where we spent the night.

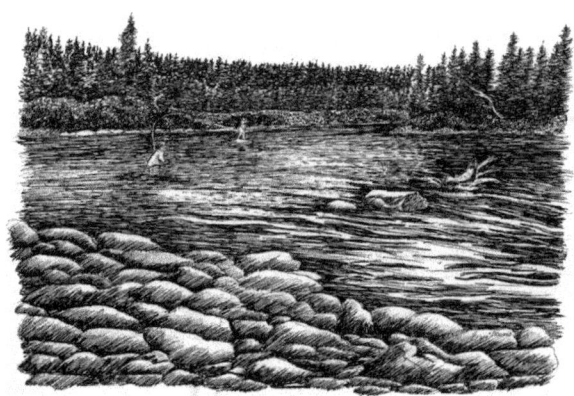

Top Pool on the Flowers River, Labrador.

A few hundred feet alongside the camp is Top Pool, one of the most perfect salmon pools I have fished. The river dumps into the rapids in a perfect "V" with rocks and boulders on the sides; it's a wonderful resting pool after the salmon has run the rapids, making it no mystery why a large number of salmon are caught there. I hooked some wonderful salmon in this pool—not my highest in numbers but my favourite nonetheless. I spent a lot of time just sitting, watching, and sketching the pool, with plans to do a watercolour of it in the future.

I fished until it got dark, and at quitting time Dan hooked one. Instead of grabbing the net and wading out, Ed yelled, "Someone stole my waders!" I looked down to discover that I had Ed's waders on, and because mine wouldn't fit him, I netted Dan's fish. After some good-natured ribbing, we retired to the camp and had a great meal that Ed prepared. *What a great memory!*

After spending the night in the cabin and having breakfast, we fished until 10:00 a.m. We then went back down the portage and met the group coming up at the bottom of the rapids. Dan decided to go with the crew from *Newfoundland Sportsman* and return to Top Pool, so Ed and I journeyed on.

The assigned pool that accompanies Top Pool is Long Beach, and that is where we headed after completing the portage and returning to the Gander River boat on the main river. Long Beach is a long, straight pool with rocks and ledges that provide holding water for a number of salmon. We knew it hadn't been fishing well; as the week progressed, only a few fish were hooked. So as I approached the pool, an interesting thought occurred to me: the air temp and colouration of the salmon suggested to me October fishing in Nova Scotia—if I were fishing my home water in October in a pool like this, I would change from summer flies to fall. With this in mind, I opened my box and found a popular fall fly, a #4 Ally's Shrimp, and tied it on. After casting it out only a few feet, a salmon slammed it! I fought it, and when Ed came out to net it and remove the fly, he just laughed and said, "I have never tied on a fly that big!" In the next hour, I hooked and landed four salmon on an Ally's Shrimp. After seeing the salmon slam it over and over, Ed became a believer in my technique.

After a while, we decided to go back to the lodge and grab a coffee and have a shower, and on the way down we met Chad and Lester, who were having a slow morning. We stopped and I gave each of them an Ally's Shrimp, telling them about the success of the fly. Chad shook his head in disbelief but tied it on. I turned and started back to the boat, but before I got there I heard, "Fish on!" It was like magic.

In the remaining days, the fall salmon lit up and those who had a fall fly did very well. That week I had an evening and a morning hooking 13 salmon—I guess the ultimate changeover on this trip was that of summer patterns to fall. In fact, I suspect the fall patterns I use in Nova Scotia will be available at the lodge during the next end-of-season fishing.

Overall, the fishing on this trip was spectacular and the Flowers River has to be the best large salmon river I have ever fished. The general consensus is that the catch-and-release policy that has been in effect for several years is the main reason, but I also attribute the number of large salmon to genetics, and those genes have been protected by the lodge's policy of no kill. *Well done!*

All good things must come to an end, and so it was with this salmon fly-fishing adventure in Labrador. We spent the last couple of days putting the lodge to bed for the winter, then loading the de Havilland Beaver floatplane and hopping aboard for the first leg of the trip home. The changeover from the hibernation of winter to summer's high-pitched activity, and then from summer back to winter was complete, and I felt fortunate to have taken part in both.

CHAPTER 7 | QUEBEC & LABRADOR

 PAYNE RIVER (QUEBEC) CHAR

by **Mark Anderson**

> Author Mark Anderson was a keen fly fisherman who was a columnist with the *Ottawa Citizen* and a *Financial Post* magazine contributor; he also often wrote about the outdoors for *Explore, Cottage Life,* and *Outdoor Canada* magazines. It was with great sadness that Mark's family announced his passing on October 16, 2014, at the age of 51. The Payne River just makes the cut for this book. Why? The Payne River Fishing Camp is situated on the 60th parallel, about 1,770 km (1,100 mi) due north of Montreal, Quebec; 240 km (150 mi) northwest of Kuujjuaq; and approximately 40 km (25 mi) upriver from the village of Kangirsuk. It's a major Arctic river that flows into Ungava Bay, the main watershed for the northwest tip of the province of Quebec. The Payne River Fishing Camp boasts that its fly fishing for Arctic char is second to none, where guests report catches of 20–30 char on a fly rod daily, which would be remarkable anywhere. Granted, the fresh char aren't necessarily in the size range of those from other Arctic rivers, but the quantity is impressive.

It's 1998, and Steve Ashton has a problem: the spin fishermen who make their way to his Payne River Fishing Camp in the Quebec Arctic are able to catch char until their shoulders ache and their reel hands cramp into palsied claws, whereas the camp's fly-fishing clients, by contrast, fare poorly. That has to change if the tiny, ten-guest operation is to remain viable and attract the type of sports who are willing and able to spend $6,000 for a week of world-class angling—which is to say, well-heeled fly fishermen.

The previous year, in 1997, Ashton invited American angler and outdoor writer Tim Jones to the camp to see if he could sort out the fly fishing. As Jones quickly discovered, however, the Payne River fjord where the camp is situated is one of the strangest places on earth—a 40-mile-long inlet from Ungava Bay, where the tides are so powerful they turn the saltwater finger into a fast-flowing river that reverses direction every six hours, causing islands and shoals to emerge as if by magic from 30 feet of water, then vanishing just as mysteriously a few hours later. Using full-sink lines and large streamers to target feeding char in current seams, Jones actually met with some success, but a year later most anglers are still spin fishing, and most fly fisherman still struggling.

**The Payne River fish camp.
(Photo credit John Beaven)**

Now Ashton reaches out yet again, this time to one of Canada's most canny and accomplished fly fishermen, the redoubtable John Beaven. Born up in Hampshire, England, in the shadow of the legendary River Test, Beaven grew up surrounded by fly fishing and its lore, and was already a passionate angler by the age of five. He immigrated to Canada in 1962 as a 20-year-old, entirely alone and determined to make a life for himself in the New World. Over the next 35 years, he would work increasingly senior jobs in a variety of technology companies, spending his leisure hours fishing the world—from New Zealand to Montana to Patagonia and yes, the Canadian Arctic. He would eventually go on to win a dozen medals in national fly-fishing competitions and captain the Canadian team at the World Fly Fishing Championships.

When Ashton approached him in 1998, his pitch was succinct and to the point: would Beaven agree to come up north and see if the Payne had what it took to be a world-class fly-fishing destination? Would he help train the hardware-chucking Inuit guides in the ways of the fly? *Indeed, he would.*

The flight from the Inuit village of Kuujjuak to the Payne River camp, high up on the 60th parallel of northern Quebec, only takes about an hour and a quarter and is a pleasant and picturesque journey on a bright summer's day, the endless expanse of rolling tundra ablaze with wildflowers and threaded through with sparkling northern rivers.

Well and good. But when the Arctic wind howls and the Twin-Otter bucks and pitches like a Rottweiler at the end of an increasingly frayed leash, that hour and a quarter can feel much, much longer—like a ride on an unfinished roller coaster, like the end of days.

And then, just when the passengers start greening at the gills, the Payne River fjord comes into view, a great gash in the earth fed by the mighty Payne River to the west, and to the east by Ungava Bay with its wicked, 50-foot tides. Shortly, the Otter banks and drops. The landing strip is not long; it's 1,100 feet (.34 km) of permafrost "paved" with a layer of palm-sized river rocks, periodically refreshed by camp maintenance crews as the existing layer melts into the underlying ice.

As construction techniques go, it's a uniquely northern bit of ad hoc engineering. Unique, too, is the fact that on certain days—including today—the runway can itself be overrun with as many as a thousand large and seemingly disinterested caribou. Not to worry. The pilot makes a pass, low and fast like an old-time barnstormer, and the caribou scatter. Then he sweeps around and comes in for the landing proper. When the turboprops power down and the Otter bumps and shudders to a stop, the passengers emerge blinking like owls in the noonday sun. Or, possibly, the midnight sun, because at 60 degrees latitude the sun never fully sets during an Ungava summer, but inscribes instead an endless arc in the cloudless, cerulean sky.

An Inuit Inuksuk (trail marker) near the Payne River fish camp.
(Photo credit John Beaven)

In short order the passengers—among them Beaven and fellow fly-rodder Paul Major—have unloaded their rods and tackle and get their first look at the Payne River Fishing Camp, situated on the bank of the fjord, 40 km (25 mi) upriver from the tiny Inuit village of Kangirsuk. The setup is modest but comfortable, with four cabins able to sleep four anglers each (even though the total number of guests never exceeds 10 at any time), a kitchen/dining room, and a common area for fly tying and socializing. The guides all hail from Kangirsuk, an hour and a half downriver by boat, though they too have their own camp quarters. Early on they weren't particularly reliable, simply because they weren't used to working day jobs, but after a couple years of training they've grown into true professionals. "They're paid well, get lots of tips, and have a hell of a lot of fun with the guests, so they appreciate the gig that they have," says Ashton. "It's the best five weeks of their year."

As for the guests, hardcore anglers all, they're far more interested in the sport than the accommodations: ahead of them, or so they hope, is a week of spectacular arctic char fishing, where 20 to 40 fish days are the rule rather than the exception. That's because each summer, char enter the fjord and concentrate in the thousands, gorging themselves on capelin, shrimp, and sand eels in advance of their fall spawning run up the Payne River and its freshwater tributaries. The char stage here, in part because the massive tides flood and flush the fjord twice daily, constantly replenishing the food supply.

It's been like this, presumably, for the last 6,500 years, ever since the Ungava Peninsula deglaciated at the end of the last ice age, allowing the Payne to flow freely to the sea. Certainly the nomadic Inuit who scraped a living from the rugged, inhospitable shores of Ungava and Hudson's Bay—following the caribou herds, harpooning beluga, and, yes, netting fish—would have been aware of the vast spawning runs of char up the Payne each fall. But it was only recently, in 1959, that the permanent Inuit settlement of Kangirsuk was established near the mouth of the fjord, and more recently still, in 1990, that these same Inuit hired Quebec adventure tour operator Steve Ashton to establish a fishing camp on the fjord and solicit angling tourism.

After a delicious dinner of grilled steak and fried char fingers with dipping sauce, the anglers are paired up with guides for their first session on the river, and it's now that Beaven starts to realize what he's up against. "It was quite clear that our Inuit guide, while a very nice fellow, wasn't that enthused about having to guide Paul and me. He'd seen fly fishermen before and knew they didn't catch anything."

They also had to adjust to the bizarre fishing schedule, which is dictated entirely by the tides. "It doesn't get dark in July, so you can fish any time of the day or night," says Beaven. "If high tide is at 3:00 a.m., you have breakfast at 2:00 a.m., and then you get in these 26-foot canoes with 50-horse motors and set out. You only have a window of an hour or two at the most to get out, and you'll be out at least 11 hours until the tide is high enough again to get back to camp."

The question was whether they would be able to prove their guide wrong, to convert him from a doubter to a fly enthusiast. As it transpired, not immediately. "We fished most of the first day and did very poorly," admits Beaven. "And since the spin fishermen were once again catching 25 char each, it just reinforced the guide's opinion that fly fishing was no good."

The problems, he figures, were several. "The guide was taking us to the same places where he would take the spin fishermen, but they use big heavy spoons that get down very quickly. Our flies were fishing too high, over the fish." Nor did it help that both Beaven and Major had set themselves up that first day with floating lines and tapered leaders, which they would later eschew for full-sink lines and short, straight leaders. Finally, their flies were all wrong. "We didn't have any information on flies and were fishing things like Woolly Buggers and Mickey Fins, which clearly weren't doing the trick."

After a frustrating 12 hours on the water, they returned to camp, licked their wounds, and considered their next move. Gutting the few char they had caught provided a valuable clue, when they discovered their stomachs full to bursting with five-inch capelin. Realizing that the flies they had been using were at least two inches too short, and also the wrong shape and colour, they spent the evening tying strips of rabbit fur onto the largest hooks they could find. They also switched to the fastest sinking lines in their arsenal in order to get their rabbit-strip flies down to where the char were feeding.

"The next day we told our guide, 'Take us close to where you think the fish are, but in water that's not quite as fast-flowing,'" says Beaven. "Immediately we were into fish, and stayed on them all day. We ended up catching about 60 between us."

As dramatic as that turnaround was, the fishing would further improve as they refined their technique and began to understand the nature of the tides, which reverses the flow of the fjord twice daily, moving and concentrating the char in the process. "From the time you start fishing until you return to camp, you're constantly on the move every half hour or so. The fishing would be red hot, and then suddenly, there'd be nothing as the tide changed. There might be a shoal just below the surface and as it emerges, suddenly it's too shallow, or too fast, or not fast enough. The bait fish move, and the char move with them."

By the third day, when they were catching 100 char per day between them, the guides were starting to come around. Beaven knew he'd won them over when, during a shore lunch on an island that emerged from under 30 feet of water at low tide, the guides quietly picked up their fly rods and began experimenting on their own. "Pretty soon we couldn't get at our rods because the guides were all using them, and even though they couldn't cast well, they were catching char after char just like we were."

Subsequent trips to the Payne by Beaven and others codified what he learned from that first exploratory expedition: the best setup for fly fishing is a 6- to 8-weight rod loaded with fast-sinking line, tipped with three or four feet of 10- to 12-pound fluorocarbon. The best flies are olive and black double bunnies made with rabbit fur, and a fly invented by Beaven's close friend and Fly Fishing Canada president Randy Taylor, made out of black and white Icelandic sheep's wool, somewhat cheekily dubbed the Sheep Shagger. "It works at least as well as the double bunny, and now when I go up I only take those two flies," says Beaven.

Dr. Royce Baxter with a fine char from the Payne River.
(Photo credit John Beaven)

Surface fishing can also be effective in the right conditions, using big, three-inch Muddler Minnows aggressively stripped. "It doesn't work all the time, but when the char smash them on the surface, it's tremendously exciting."

Spin fishermen, meanwhile, continue to have great sport on the Payne using a variety of spoons, including Pixies, Daredevles, Williams Wobblers, Moosehooks—even Rapala Minnows that have had their treble hooks replaced with single barbless hooks. Spoons and plugs 2–3.5 inches in length seem to work best.

Whether pitching flies or hardware, the sport is unsurpassed. "The Payne doesn't have the largest char, with the vast majority being in the 5- to 8-pound range, but there is nowhere else in

North America that has anywhere near the quantity," says Beaven. "They're silver, sea-run fish, and incredibly strong. By the end of the day your muscles are just burning."

And if you ever get tired of hammering the char, there are other options as well: two hours upriver from the camp, you can catch brook trout up to 10 pounds, as well as lake trout to double that size, in the freshwater rapids of the Payne River proper.

Throw in the spectacular, otherworldly landscape and regular sightings of caribou, wolf, musk ox, and beluga whales, and it's easy to see why the Payne is now attracting adventurous anglers from throughout the world, and is widely regarded as the best Arctic char fishery in North America—whether you're fly fishing or not.

| CO-EDITOR'S NOTE | After reading Mark Anderson's article about fly fishing for Arctic char in the Payne River, I had to admit I had doubts that fishing could possibly be this great anywhere on earth. I wondered whether Mark had gotten carried away with Arctic hyperbole. Consequently, it was incumbent on me to verify the accuracy of Mark's article by getting a second opinion from an experienced Canadian fishing guide, C. Perry Munro, who has as much experience fly fishing for char, brook trout, and Atlantic salmon as anybody I know. I owe a sincere apology to Mark for being a bit skeptical—he didn't exaggerate one bit according to what Perry said because this place has all the appearances of heaven on earth for char-fishing enthusiasts!   —Duane S. Radford |

CHAPTER 8

Yukon

Yukon Fishing

by **Duane S. Radford**

Much like many Americans dream of driving the Alaska Highway, many Canadians pine for a trip to the Yukon, where the world's last great gold rush occurred from 1896 to 1899, because the history of the Yukon is so steeped in romance. Authors like Robert Service and Jack London have forever immortalized the lure of the North in the hearts of many would-be adventurers from around the world. What many travellers don't know is that the Yukon has some outstanding fishing and unparalleled scenery found nowhere else on earth, and getting there is becoming easier each year. Major commercial airlines connect Yukon's capital city of Whitehorse directly with Vancouver, Calgary, Edmonton, Ottawa, and Yellowknife. Europeans, particularly Germans, have long had a love affair with the wilds of the Yukon, and Condor features weekly service from Frankfurt, Germany, to Whitehorse from June to September.

The Yukon Territory is 483,450 square kilometres (186,661 square miles) in area, larger than the state of California—or Belgium, Denmark, Germany, and the Netherlands combined. On June 21st, the date of the summer solstice when the sun never sets in some parts of the Yukon, you can read a book in the wee hours. The midnight sun makes for long days and lingering sunsets that last for hours, not minutes, and the extended sunlight is incredibly energizing, making most people feel young and invigorated, not to mention the unending daylight makes for wonderful karma.

Yukon Tourism bills the Yukon as "Larger than Life," and for those seeking a wilderness fishing adventure, the Yukon territory has them in spades—there's probably no other spot in Canada that ranks higher as a bucket-list vacation than a trip to the Yukon. Much of its most spectacular wilderness is protected by a network of national and territorial parks and protected areas and is the largest eco-region in the world. It's top of mind for many American, Canadian, and European tourists due largely to the ongoing romance of the Klondike Gold Rush and the dream to drive the famed Alaska Highway, which was completed in 1942—due to the threat of a Japanese invasion in Alaska—and was opened to the public in 1948. The highway is currently paved its entire length and remains a very popular drive, emblematic of the phrase "North to Alaska."

The spell of the gold rush was forever cast in the works of Jack London and Robert Service, whose writings immortalized those halcyon days in the late 1800s. Nowadays, if you take in the Frantic Follies show at the Westmark Hotel in Whitehorse or watch the dance hall girls' cancan show at Diamond Tooth Gerties Gambling Hall in Dawson City, you'll be taken back in time with period vaudeville acts that are highly entertaining even today. It's the aura of the famous gold rush that separates vacations to the Yukon from those of the Northwest Territories and Nunavut.

Tincup Lake Wilderness Lodge.

During my fishing trips to far-off destinations North of Sixty, I've experienced a range of emotions in these last Canadian frontiers. The Northwest Territories is an immense, almost frightening raw wilderness—of seemingly endless brooding forests, mountains, lakes, and streams—with a visceral edge to it. Unlike Nunavut or the Yukon, that edge may be stark and foreboding. In contrast, I find Nunavut to be hauntingly eerie and sometimes intimidating because it's so isolated, rugged, and barren. The thought that often crosses my mind there is: *how could anybody find his or her way around the barren grounds, let alone actually survive on the sweeping tundra—even in the summer, never mind the winter?* Hence, the barren lands of Nunavut are aptly named.

Yukon, on the other hand, is a land of seemingly endless, romantic postcard landscapes, with its rugged, majestic mountains and numerous way points steeped in history. Yukon is also blessed with many thoroughly modern amenities for the wayward traveller, unlike the Northwest Territories or Nunavut—although

CHAPTER 8 | YUKON

Yellowknife, the capital of the Northwest Territories, is every bit as cosmopolitan as Whitehorse, the capital of the Yukon.

Over the past several years, air connections to the Yukon have changed dramatically with the expansion of Air North flights, a long-standing regional carrier based out of Whitehorse, to/from Calgary/Edmonton, Alberta and Vancouver, and British Columbia, as well as Air Canada flights from Calgary and Vancouver. There's even a once-a-week flight from Frankfurt, Germany, on Condor from May to September. If you'd prefer to drive the Alaska Highway the distance between Edmonton, Alberta's capital city and Whitehorse, it's 2,013 km (1,251 mi) or 2,676 km (1,663 mi) from Vancouver to Whitehorse. If you travel by vehicle, you'll be pleasantly surprised with the modern roads that cover a good portion of the Yukon Territory, many of which are paved. Campgrounds are spread out, so you should be able to find one in a convenient location, and most overnight campgrounds have fishing access sites for you to wet a line.

If there's anything that stands out about fishing destinations in the Yukon, it is the sheer grandeur of the lakes and streams in the territory. They are often in breathtaking places, so even if the fishing happens to be slow, you'll feel satisfied with the experience. Actually, fishing is usually

Fly fishing on the Aishiak River, Yukon.

great because the Yukon offers an abundance of fish and fishing opportunities, with light local fishing pressure. Another unique feature of the Yukon is the variety of game fish compared with the Northwest Territories and Nunavut. Yukon is home to northern pike, chum salmon, lake trout, kokanee and sockeye salmon, Chinook salmon, rainbow trout, steelhead, Arctic char, Dolly Varden, bull trout, Coho salmon, lake whitefish, mountain whitefish, Inconnu, burbot, and Arctic grayling. For more details, I recommend picking up *Yukon Freshwater Fishes* (2009), a free publication that introduces Yukoners and visitors to the various freshwater species of fish of the territory.

Grizzly bear sow and cubs along the Alaska Highway, Yukon.

Several full-service fishing lodges and other lodges provide boats and accommodations, and most lodges are accessible by floatplane only, although some such as the Dalton Trail Lodge are accessible by vehicle. It isn't necessary to hire a fishing guide or stay in a lodge as there are lots of fine campgrounds throughout the Yukon backcountry. If you want to experience some extraordinary fishing, however, you might want to stay at a lodge and/or hire a fishing guide. A word of caution, though, if you're going to do it yourself: black bears and grizzly bears are ubiquitous in the Yukon. It's not uncommon to see both species in riparian zones (in particular) or in the high country. I've seen as many as half a dozen grizzly bears on a given day without even looking for them—they can be that numerous. Yukon actually boasts that it is home to 25 percent of Canada's grizzly bears, so you should take precautions to avoid encounters with both black and grizzly bears, which can be very dangerous.

With numerous lakes and streams, you can catch fish with spinning gear or by fly fishing in the Yukon. One of the best resources is the online "Fishing on Yukon Time—A Guide to Fishing in Yukon" brochure for those not acquainted with this territory, available at the following link:

www.env.gov.yk.ca/hunting-fishing-trapping/wherefish.php

This handy brochure outlines not only the kind of fish in the Yukon, but also how to catch them; it even features a map of the Yukon showing where to find the most popular species. A chapter in the brochure called "Fish and First Nations" is a must-read. While there's no specific reference that First Nations people are concerned about "catch-and-release fishing" in this brochure, it illustrates that fish are still a staple food item for many indigenous people who may not always agree with fishing for fun. As such, be sensitive to this issue and limit your catch, because it is easy to catch many fish during a trip to the Yukon.

Wade Sali with a lake trout from the Kathleen River, Yukon.

Over the past decade, several fishing guide/outfitters have set up shop in the Yukon in addition to the already existing fishing lodges. Go online if you'd like to make a booking with a guide/outfitter that provides a range of services; the following link gives details regarding costs, terms, and booking information:

http://bit.ly/yukon-wild-fishing

While there is no single online source for fishing lodges in the Yukon, the following lodges were in operation at the time of publishing:

DALTON TRAIL LODGE
www.daltontrail.com

GRIZZLY CREEK LODGE
www.grizzlycreeklodge.com

INCONNU LODGE
www.inconnulodge.com

KLUANE WILDERNESS LODGE
www.kluanelodge.com

WOLF LAKE LODGE
www.wolflake.ca

RUBY RANGE WILDERNESS & FISHING LODGE
www.rubyrangelodge.com

TINCUP WILDERNESS LODGE
www.tincup-lodge.com

I've been to the Dalton Trail Lodge, Grizzly Creek Lodge, Kluane Wilderness Lodge, and Tincup Wilderness Lodge and enjoyed outstanding fishing for various species during these trips. Each of the lodges has its own unique characteristics; some even have super-size fish not generally advertised, so check out the lodges online for details about the nature of fish species present, which is variable. For transportation, some of the lodges offer fly-outs or use the main lodge as a base from which to travel to various destinations by boat and vehicle.

As a last note, I'd be remiss not to say that if you are planning a fishing trip to the Yukon, you should stay for a vacation in this truly remarkable Canadian territory so steeped in history. The Yukon has numerous tourist attractions, excellent accommodations, many fine restaurants, and a back-country charm found nowhere else in Canada.

Gold was discovered near Dawson City on August 16, 1896; Whitehorse was but a small settlement on the banks of the Yukon

River at the time. As the largest city west of Winnipeg, Manitoba, and north of Seattle, Washington, Dawson City had a population of about 30,000 at the turn of the century near the end of the gold rush. By comparison, Yukon has a population of just over 31,000 people today, almost identical to that of 1900, with a population of about 25,000 in Whitehorse, the staging area for most guided fishing trips and jaunts to fishing lodges in the Yukon (details regarding angling licences in the Yukon are found in the first chapter of this book).

As the saying goes, "You haven't seen the Yukon until you've visited Dawson City," so mark it down as a must-do part of your vacation, along with your fishing trip.

An Embarrassment of Fishes

by Patrick Walsh

> Patrick Walsh shares his fishing adventures on a trip with the venerable *Outdoor Canada* Fishing Editor Gord Pyzer at Wolf Lake, Yukon, a remote fly-in lake east of Whitehorse out of Wolf Lake Lodge. Patrick is the (sometimes) self-deprecating editor of *Outdoor Canada* magazine and an award-winning writer who has fished across northern Canada. Co-editor Duane S. Radford spent an enjoyable week with Patrick at Plummer's Arctic Lodges Great Bear Lake Lodge and at the Tree River Lodge, and shared in the moment when Patrick dived into the Arctic Ocean as a rite of passage. Patrick is no shrinking violet, and he's a keen angler who thoroughly enjoys adventures in Canada's North Country.

On the Yukon's remote and wild Wolf River, expect to tackle as many feisty Arctic grayling as you can possibly handle. And then some.

A triple-header on Wolf River grayling with Ted Cawkwell (L), Patrick Walsh (middle) and Gord Pyzer (R).

I'm not a great fly fisherman; I know that. I'm okay at best, but I aspire to improve. I have a stack of books about technique for this and that manner of catching fish on the fly, and I have a vise for tying. Oh, to tie flies. How cool would that be? I mean, to catch fish with something you spun up with your very own hands—that's making the connection. All I need, really, is the time to do it, or so I tell myself. I certainly know the satisfaction of catching fish with my own creation.

A couple of years back on the Ganaraska River, I caught my biggest-ever Ontario chinook with a roe bag I tied myself, chock full of eggs I'd harvested the previous year from a rainbow trout. I let that big old beat-up chinook go, too. He'd played his part twice over, having both spewed his milt and fed my ego, and deserved to expire of his own volition.

Such fly-fishing hero moments are few and far between in my patch of southern Ontario, however—at least for me. Oh yes, I've hunted and caught middling browns with dries on the Grand, which was very enjoyable, and I've caught smallies with streamers on the Saugeen—the latter, admittedly, thanks to one of my many fly-fishing mentors, Mike Verhoef. And I know there are other challenges awaiting me, like landing a monster muskie on the fly.

But such challenges require hard work—and time. In late June, 2009, I wasn't looking for hard work, and I didn't have weeks and weeks to pattern my quarry. But I did want to catch fish—a lot of fish—and on the fly at that. Fortunately, salvation was at hand. Months earlier, my pal Ted Cawkwell urged me and *Outdoor Canada*'s fishing editor, Gord Pyzer, to join him up in the

Yukon at Wolf Lake Lodge, about 177 km (110 air miles) southeast of Whitehorse, up and over the rugged, snow-capped Englishman's Range. "Man, you gotta get up there," he told me over the phone.

Now, I've followed Ted to parts north before on the promise of awesome fishing and was amply rewarded. Namely, when he ran Milton Lake Lodge in remote northern Saskatchewan a few years back, I caught my personal best fish, a 37-pound lake trout. Naturally, I was all ears.

The promise this time? No end to easy fish on the fly, including Arctic grayling, pike, and—once again—lunker lake trout. Ted was particularly jazzed about the lakers. He's friends with the lodge owners, Wes and Michelle Walker, and had joined them the previous fall after their fly-in operation had shut down for the season. The lake trout bite, he said, "was just insane."

And so I signed on.

As it turned out, the laker action when Gord and I visited was okay, but not out-of-this-world fantastic as Ted had described, no doubt largely due to the bouncing barometer. And since I'm not an entirely seasoned fly angler, flinging weightless bits of nothing against hard northern winds and into grey, choppy water seemed distinctly out of the question. So much for catching my first-ever laker on the fly.

Sure, maybe I'd have a fighting chance if I were to return during the fall spawn, with the fish congregating on the lake's handful of shoals, but not in late June, with the trout already scattered and on the move. While Wolf isn't a giant lake—21 km (13 mi) long and 5 km (3 mi) across at its widest point—it did seem to me that trolling hardware and covering lots of water was the wisest proposition for guaranteeing some fish in the boat. Who would even try to catch lakers on the fly at that time of year anyway?

Frank Dale and John Horsey, that's who. The two British guests deep-dunked tiny chironomid patterns to put up a number of trout, including Frank's stated goal of landing a 10-plus-pound fish. And what a sweet moment that was, just minutes past midnight on our fourth evening, the sun hanging on the horizon and the water as though it were glass—a welcome respite from the earlier blustery, grey weather. Gord and I had been trolling nearby in the broad, shallow bay at the south end of the lake, and had just motored up to their 14-foot aluminum when Frank's rod bent. Talk about patience and fish smarts personified—and rewarded, complete with a nice, silver 11-pounder.

Gord Pyzer with one of many grayling.

In the end, I caught a few trout out on the main lake too, albeit using my big-ass baitcaster, 30-pound braid, and an ever-changing assortment of spoons and swimbaits. The best producer was a modest, glow-coloured #3 Syclops, which I tied on after the Brits figured it was worth downsizing from my hefty Half Waves and Len Thompsons to at least try to match the pin minnows two of their trout had coughed up. I also tried trolling big streamers on a sink-tip line, the fly tactic favoured by the lodge, but had no luck.

My experience notwithstanding, the potential clearly exists to catch big trout with a fly rod. Some months after returning home, I got in contact with Lars Jessup, a fisheries technician with Environment Yukon. A former fishing guide, he recalls speaking with other guides who boasted of Wolf lakers up to 30 pounds on the fly, putting the lake in the company of the Yukon's other renowned laker destinations, such as Wellesley, Tincup, and Toobally. "Anecdotally," Jessup told me, "Wolf Lake is known for good lake trout fishing and large lake trout."

The most recent survey conducted by Environment Yukon appears to back up this contention. Of the 21 fish netted, tagged, and released in 2005, the average size was nine and a half pounds. Says Jessup, "I think it's safe to say that this is larger than the average from most other lakes."

Since taking over the 32-year-old lodge from the original owner in 1998, Wes and Michelle have themselves caught big trout. And so have their guests, they say, collectively landing roughly 30 fish topping 40 pounds every season, and another five or so tipping the scales at more than 50 pounds. The record so far under their watch is a 58-pound monster, hauled in nine years ago by a visiting angler from California.

The Walkers credit several factors for the health of the fishery, not the least of which is their catch-and-release policy and the low volume of guests: 50 at most make their way to the lodge each season. The fact there's no road access helps too; the nearest town, the 500-member T'lingit community of Teslin, is 44 air miles (71 km) to the southwest. And because Yukon's fishing regulations list Wolf Lake as a so-called conservation water, barbless hooks are mandatory and a slot limit is in place, demanding the release of any fish between 26 and 39 inches in length.

As for my particular visit, though, the bottom line was that I was unable to fly-fish for lake trout. And by that I don't mean trolling, but actually casting and working my fly back in, striving to provoke a strike. That's what I really wanted to do. To me, the laker fishing with hardware, along with sojourns for pike in neighbouring Wolverine and May Lakes, had become the sideshows, the mere warm-ups to what I hoped would be the big event: tossing bits of thread, hair, and feather for Arctic grayling on the Wolf River.

Or more specifically, catching them on dries.

Gord Pyzer with the largest laker taken by Patrick's fishing gang from Wolf Lake.

My terms of reference for Arctic grayling fishing are slim at best. And perhaps skewed. Actually, my first and only grayling experience prior to fishing the Wolf might well have spoiled me. It was on the Sulky River, a quick fly-out from Plummer's Great Bear Lake Lodge on the Dease Arm of the NWT's Great Bear Lake. We caught, released, and ate grayling at will, almost to the point of routine. Almost. You just can't get bored about that splashing smack on a dry, the quivering bend in the rod, and the satisfaction of bringing such a beautiful fish to hand.

Unlike the relatively tiny Sulky, however, the Wolf River is much broader, with a stiffer current and many more fish-holding stretches—at least until it spills over the first set of Class III rapids as it wends its way 140 km (87 mi) west and south to join the Nisutlin River and empty into Teslin Lake. And unlike the Sulky, the Wolf comes complete with a growing reputation as a top Arctic grayling fishery, offering up fantastic numbers, as well as true trophies approaching the four-and-a-half-pound range.

One of the Wolf River's boosters is Dutch angler Hans van Klinken, a renowned fly tier, author, photographer, and freelance journalist. Perhaps his most famous pattern, the Klinkhamer Special, is said to be just deadly on grayling. I wrote to him to verify his contention that the Wolf reigns supreme, but he didn't respond. No mind. I then heard about John Wilson, personified as Mr. Angling on British TV. According to him, the Wolf "is arguably the best place for grayling on the planet." And in the Sept. 11, 2007, issue of the U.K.'s *Angling Times*, he lauds the river as "grayling heaven."

Certainly for an angler such as I, it was heaven. Remember my admission that I'm not an entirely efficient fly fisherman, prone to few hero moments? Well, on the Wolf River I was a constant hero, catching grayling almost nonstop, alternating between dries and nymphs depending on the changing mood of the fish. And my catches were not in the dozens, but in the hundreds, which was all the more remarkable considering the grayling had only just begun to enter the river from their winter redoubts on Wolf Lake. According to Michelle, the fishing only gets better throughout the summer.

The grayling were so ravenous, I was a fly-fishing hero even when I didn't want to be, such as when I was messing around trying to unravel pesky wind knots. Three times I caught fish as my suspended fly skipped along the water's surface, mere inches away, while I fumbled with chilled fingers to undo the latest intelligence test of a knot. Through the gin-clear water, I could even see the fish hovering in the current just downstream of my submerged lower half, treating me as though I was nothing more than a piece of structure.

In short, I caught so many grayling not because of any particular skill on my part, but by mere dint of geography. These are truly wild fish inhabiting a remote slice of pristine wilderness, completely alien to the concept of fishing pressure. Theirs is a world of rugged mountain vistas and white spruce forests, a world shared with the likes of beaver, moose, woodland caribou, and golden eagle—not man. All of this, of course, adds to the overall appeal and infectious nature of wading the river, even for guests otherwise determined to catch a lunker laker back out on Wolf Lake. "They come for the lake trout," says Michelle, "but become grayling lovers by the time they leave."

Yes, the Arctic grayling were a big draw for me, in particular the chance to catch them, one after the other, on dry flies. Anticipating, watching, and feeling the take was pure fly-fishing bliss—nonstop bliss. But I'd be lying if I told you that catching upward of 200 fish a day was the highlight of the three days I spent on the Wolf River. Sometimes, all it takes is just one fish, an off-script interloper, to change the game, if only for a moment. And sometimes, that brief, unexpected change-up can make for the defining catch, the fish that trumps all when it comes to summing up your time on the water, whether it's an afternoon on a local pond or six days at a remote, mountain-cradled Yukon fish camp. And I caught just that fish, on my second-to-last day, in the last place I would have expected.

Not that I should have been surprised. I mean, why wouldn't lake trout abandon their main-lake haunts and venture down the Wolf River chasing grayling? It made total sense afterwards, but when Ted first started freaking out about a giant slashing through the pool in front of me, lake trout was not the fish I envisaged. For sure, I thought he had seen the biggest grayling yet, some four-plus-pound bruiser, so big its girth was evident even through the shimmering current.

"Get it!" I yelled back to Ted.

"But I only have a five-weight ..."

Huh?

"... and a box of nymphs!"

Wah?

"It's a big laker!" Ted yelled again, having interpreted my furrowed brow.

Suddenly, it all made sense.

Oh.

Ohhh!

The thing is, I was also fishing a five-weight. And an ever-shortening 5x tapered leader. That was cool with the two-pound-max grayling in the stiff current, but a big, bad trout on the feed? Not so much.

Screw it, I thought. *This fish is mine.*

From there, I kind of went on autopilot. All I recall is remembering I had a big saltwater streamer in my vest, a Baja

Baitfish I'd bought back in Ontario at Bass Pro Shops, more or less on a whim, thinking it would work a treat on Yukon pike. Hell, it was meant for fooling bonito, dorado, sailfish, yellowtail, and other predators of the sea, so why not pike? I can't tell you how it worked on Yukon pike, because I plumb neglected to switch over to my nine-weight and tie it on when Gord and I were slaying them with hardware earlier in the week on Wolverine and May. But I can tell you how it fared with the big lake trout.

The first cool thing about this fish story is that I couldn't see the fish. I could see that Ted was as excited as all get out, because he actually could see it, slashing through the very pool we'd just started mining for our latest score of gullible grayling. But with the flat light and low sun, all I saw was the day's endless pesky cloud cover shimmering in the current. No mind; as soon as Ted said he was out of the running, I just had to step up and take my best shot at catching the marauding laker, under-gunned as I was.

As mentioned, it was as though I'd flipped on the autopilot. Without missing a beat (okay, I'm for once romanticizing my angling prowess here, but it really did come down this way), I snipped off my tiny beaded nymph (the grayling had stopped rising at that point), retrieved the Baja Baitfish from the streamer box in my vest, tied it on, and unfurled.

Unfurled.

I wish.

Let's back up a tad.

Rather, I excitedly made a sloppy cast, plopping the big Baja in the pool somewhat near where Ted said the laker was merrily feeding, about three metres crosscurrent from my position.

No mind. Strip, strip, strip, strip.

Nothing.

Cast again. A bit better this time.

Strip, strip, strip, strip.

Again, nothing.

Last time lucky (you can say that, in retrospect, when your last cast connects).

And oh yeah, it did. Cast, strip, strip—BOOM!

"You got her!"

Ted was again freaking out, probably because he had never lost sight of the fish, standing as he was opposite me on the pool, the bad light to his advantage, directing my every toss of the line.

Had him I did. Luckily, he was apparently unaware of that rather salient point, and instead swam towards me—and shallower water—nearly beaching himself alongside the submerged foliage of a mid-river island (thank you seasonal high water) as I battled to keep a slight bend in the rod. Perhaps he thought he had nothing more than the sharp dorsal of a hapless grayling sticking in his craw. Who knows? But his solution to the situation was to swim downriver, following the shallow edge of the flooded island. And that's when Ted and I knew we had him. Rather, that's when we knew it was our only chance to land the fish before he rounded the tip of the island, got whisked away by the converging river currents, and broke off.

Now, I've already credited Ted with spotting this fish in the first place, but I also must dispense no end of thanks for his skill as a net man. Namely, he had the wherewithal, while I was coaching the big laker away from the fast water, to grab the cradle out of our moored boat, follow me downstream, and slyly scoop up the fish before he even knew he was about to become the subject of my latest angling hero photo.

In the end, he wasn't a huge trout, weighing somewhere between 15 and 20 pounds, but he was definitely my biggest fish of the trip. And as far as I was concerned, he was a genuine trophy, something I thought had eluded me this trip.

My first-ever lake trout on the fly.

CHAPTER 8 | YUKON

Patrick with his first-ever laker on a fly.

GETTING THERE: Air Canada and Air North offer daily flights to Whitehorse from Vancouver and Calgary. Air North also operates flights from Edmonton. From Whitehorse, it's a one-hour floatplane jaunt into Wolf Lake; the flight is included with a stay at Wolf Lake Wilderness Lodge, the only operation on the lake.

ACCOMMODATIONS: The lodge has four private, comfortable cabins, housing up to three guests each, complete with en suite bathrooms and hot running water. They serve "five-star wilderness cuisine" three times daily in the main lodge (expect to put on weight), and you can enjoy sundowners in the screened-in, heated gazebo bar, which also features a hot tub.

WHEN TO GO: Four-, six-, eight-, and 10-day stays are offered in June and July only. The lake trout, pike, and whitefish action is said to be fairly consistent throughout the two months, but the Arctic grayling opportunities on the Wolf River typically don't kick into high gear until late June when the fish return from their winter vacations in Wolf Lake.

PERMITS: Visitors to the Yukon will need a non-resident's fishing licence, available at the lodge.

GEAR: Along with four-stroke equipped 14-foot Lunds, the lodge provides all necessary spinfishing tackle. If you're like me, though, you'll want to bring along your own favourite laker and pike rigs. For lake trout, try #3 Syclops in glow, red-body Pixees, and big, hollow-bodied swimbaits; the lodge has a decent selection of spoons. For pike, you can't go wrong with #5 Aglias, spinnerbaits, and swimbaits. As for the grayling, a five-weight setup should give you enough backbone for the strong current, while practically any small dry fly or beaded nymph will do the trick. You'll of course also want a camera, as well as insect repellent, sunscreen, lip balm, and polarized sunglasses. For those who must remain tethered to the world back home, the lodge provides Internet access via satellite.

CLOTHING: Wolf Lake is North of Sixty, so arrive fully prepared for all manner of weather, especially earlier in the season. Layers are recommended, and don't forget your rain gear. Also bring gloves, a hat, a toque, and warm, waterproof footwear.

MORE INFO: Wolf Lake Wilderness Lodge, www.wolflake.ca; (306) 873-7733 (September 15 to June 1); (250) 483-6919 (June 1 to September 15). Tourism Yukon, www.travelyukon.com; 1-800-661-0494.

CHAPTER 8 | YUKON

OPERATION S.N.A.F.U.

by Jeff Dewsbury

> "Haunted, taunted, and ultimately redeemed in the bug-thick bush country of the Yukon. One angler's pursuit of a boyhood dream..." is how Vancouver, British Columbia, freelance writer Jeff Dewsbury describes his do-it-yourself trip in the Yukon wilderness with some of his longtime fishing buddies. Jeff lived his dream during this Yukon adventure while fishing for pike, lake whitefish, grayling, and lake trout in what he describes as "angling Eden." Military buffs will be familiar with the term Snafu (probably in more descriptive terms than would be suitable for this book), so some of Jeff's humourous adventures related to his Yukon trips will no doubt be categorized as "misadventures" in their minds.

It's unpatriotic to curse a national symbol. But after hauling three boats over the third gnat-infested beaver dam of the day, the harsh words are queued up on the tip of my tongue, waiting for a bug-free millisecond to hit the air. The ghosts of Snafu Lake are definitely on the wind. I can even picture the Canadian military engineers who named this enigmatic lake after the acronym for "Situation Normal: All Fouled Up"—they're either chuckling at our efforts, or scoffing at how mild our situation is compared to the mosquito-clouded hell they endured back in the late 1940s. How bad was it for them? I can only imagine what it was like to build a 100-km road through this stretch of Yukon wilderness. No wonder they also gave another nearby lake the name Tarfu—the acronym for "Things Are Really Fouled Up." The question now is, how bad will it get for us?

Like a lot of boys, I spent hours tromping along the banks of local creeks in my youth when I should have been cutting the lawn. Dog-eared fishing compilations such as *Angler's Bible* and

Trout Fisherman's Digest played a big part in feeding my early angling addiction. Grainy photos of plaid-shirted men holding monster pike by the gills were the mainstay of these publications. I'd sit by the fire in my home near Ontario's Georgian Bay and wonder if I would ever be that guy landing a lunker, complete with a pipe resting on my lips, a floatplane in the background, and a shore lunch on the go.

Even with all the worn metaphors and tourist brochure hyperbole about the Yukon—the midnight sun, the gold rush, and so on—my childhood awe over that part of the country has remained, as has my curiosity. So when three fishing buddies tell me they're heading to a chain of pike-filled lakes in the Yukon, I'm all ears. And when they say two of the lakes are the mysteriously named Snafu and Tarfu, I just know I have to go.

When we arrive in Whitehorse, I rush off the plane with all the gusto of a raging river, eager to get the show on the road and start living my boyhood dream. Our unofficial host is Don Flinn, who exemplifies the pace that suits these waters best. Right away, he sets my clock straight, telling me it's time to slow down. In Don's world, when you go to a lake and someone else is fishing there, it's too busy; try spot number two. In the unlikely event someone is in that spot too, keep going. After all, you've got all night thanks to the midnight sun. In June, locals might not even leave the house until 10:00 p.m. for an evening of fishing.

Don is proud of the size of his playground and, like many of the people lured to the Yukon, he's somewhat of an evangelist for the kind of life he leads in the wide-open spaces. He says his son once asked him who their neighbour was. Don's reply? "Your neighbour is someone from the same watershed as you."

Now enlightened, I'm looking forward to the fishing even more. It's tempting to focus on personal statistics when fishing in bountiful waters, but playing the numbers can be a fool's game, and I'm wary of developing a forest-for-the-trees syndrome. At least my three companions—Brian, Mitch, and Phil—have made this trip many times before, and following their lead takes a lot of guesswork out of the equation.

Regrettably, one piece of wisdom I didn't glean before reaching our base cabin on Atlin Lake was the foresight to pack a mosquito net. While Mitch quickly digs into Phil for bringing his "princess net" again, I would gladly trade the buzzing in my ears for the sound of taunts any day. "What's the problem, mate? Mosquitoes getting to you?" Phil teases back in his rollicking British accent as Mitch slinks deeper into his sleeping bag, fighting vainly against the feasting hordes drawn to the heat of the cabin.

Somewhere, the ghosts are surely beginning to laugh.

The next day, we're forced to drag our three car boats—and outboards—over a series of beaver dams to nearby Snafu Lake. It seems like a small price to pay, however, to access each new tier of this fishing Eden. I even begin to tolerate the water spilling into my waders and the DEET pooling in every pore of my skin, not to mention the extra gnat protein I'm inhaling. And after all, we're going fishing, not carving a road through the bush.

The author and fishing buddy Phil Cann push over a beaver dam in the Snafu Lake watershed.

Officially, Snafu is regarded as a single lake, but that doesn't accurately describe the enormity and character of this body of water. There are numerous waterways spilling from bay to bay, forming a maze of smaller lakes, backwaters, streams, and islands, with every nook and cranny seemingly bursting with fish.

As we make our way to the highest "lake" in the chain, we pass an impossibly pastoral scene—a peaceful, clear-water bay beside a stony river, merrily babbling beside an abandoned cabin—that encapsulates all the romantic notions of the Yukon. Putting any thoughts of winter (and bugs) aside, it's difficult to imagine anyone packing up the canoe and leaving this paradise.

The best way to start off a fishing trip is with a can't-miss proposition, so we spend the morning pitching heavy flies that look like animated hair pieces crossbred with Christmas ornaments. We don't need Kreskin with us to foretell that the pike will chase these mutations as though they haven't eaten in 100 years. The trick is to get the fly out in front of the double-digit fish, those lazy lurkers with shoulders, and away from the reckless youth and their hopped-up hormones.

The author hoists one of his numerous pike from Snafu Lake.

One curious trait of the pike we encounter is the propensity of the trophy fish to move in for a better look when one of their brethren has been hooked—this when I'm accustomed to seeing all living life forms flee the crime scene. I'm prone to anthropomorphisms, so the image of a smug pike dispassionately getting a front-row seat for his buddy's potential demise seems darkly comical.

Mitch, who had witnessed this type of pike behaviour on previous trips, is all business. And when I hook a lesser specimen, he gets his fly out of the water, up in the air, and over to the action as soon as possible. Using this tactic, he manages to hook a number of granddaddy lookers-on emerging from the shadows.

Eventually, we tire of the pike and their brash ways. Opting for a more discreet quarry, we shuttle over to the extensive marl and gravel flats on the lee side of a nearby island, trading in our cumbersome hair-hat flies and weighty rods in favour of a more refined presentation: slender, natural-looking size 14 to 18 nymphs, longer, lighter leaders, and the rods to match.

Here, we sight-fish for whitefish, which could be likened to fishing the flats for bonefish, albeit without the knuckle-busting runs. We slap on indicators, which keep the flies at the desired depth but don't really betray the fish's bite, and the take is so light with these soft-mouthed cruisers that the indicator barely moves when the sparse halfback nymph is sucked in.

The wind whips across our little flat just enough to impart an enticing action on the fly, but the chop on the water also plays games with my eyes as I strain to read the drifting indicator's movements. "I always set the hook before the indicator moves," Mitch tells me as he surveys his open fly box. "And I never fish for whitefish unless I can see them."

This turns out to be valuable advice. It takes awhile to get accustomed to lightly lifting my rod when the shadow of a fish pauses below my indicator, but I'm soon steadily hooking into the little gems along with the other guys. My newfound gentle touch makes this a day of extreme contrasts, a yin and yang of angling, where the soft sips of the whitefish counterbalance the suicidal tendencies of their reckless pike neighbours. The promise of this angling Eden has been met. Take that, ghosts.

The following morning, we change gears yet again by going down to the valley floor to test the Lubbock River, which snakes between Atlin and Little Atlin Lakes. The Lubbock is one of those magical little rivers that reveals another side of its character around every bend. Grassy banks, deep pockets amid babbling rapids, and long, tree-lined runs are some of its most striking features. Best of all, the Arctic grayling have moved in for their brief spring spawn.

Our expectations are high, as the fish are rising everywhere, even as the warm sun surrenders to a heavy downpour. Yet the fish reject our litany of flies, as if the ghosts have whispered a warning to beware the fur and feathers that fall from the sky. A few carefree souls fail to heed the admonition—rarely can an entire gauntlet of fish ignore a high-floating orange Stimulator or a properly dead-drifted Hare's Ear. Still, the spectacle of so many rising fish simply rejecting our offerings is almost too much to take.

Expectations dictate the success of any angling experience. While one or two silvery little fish will put a smile on my face during a mid-February outing for coastal cutthroat, anything less than continuous action in this paradise is disheartening. So I head back to the cabin with a scowl on my face and 52 new mosquito bites, the rainstorm having purged me of my bug repellent. The best way to ease such bitterness is to be handed an unexpected gift, and my mood softens when the ghosts make a peace offering of sorts.

Phil Cann casts into Atlin Lake across from the dome-like Mount Minto.

Atlin Lake, which straddles the B.C.-Yukon border, is one of those deep, volatile bodies of water that trollers love and fly anglers avoid. Smooth-sided Mount Minto towers over it, looking like a northern version of Australia's famed Ayers Rock, and it's common for waves to pound the lake's rocky shoals for days at a time in the spring. But on the evening after the Lubbock grayling shunned our flies, Atlin is as flat as yesterday's beer.

With restored hope, I cast into the half-light of the lingering evening as a thick wall of fog crawls across the water towards me. Most major faiths have their own term for a transcendental state, where the soul seemingly detaches from the cares of the body. If angling carries with it an element of spirituality—it does, after all, involve faith—then I'm definitely approaching rapture.

The contrast between the sliver of orange topping the trees to my right and the encroaching fog to my left acts as my only clock. When the orange is gone and the white air is close enough to hit with a cast, it will be time to find the path back to the cabin. Until then, the short tugs of grayling meeting the little olive Woolly Bugger on the end of my tippet count down the last few minutes of usable light. The frustrations of Lubbock already seem like a rumour I heard long ago.

Uncooperative fish and ravenous bugs notwithstanding, if there's one black mark on my Yukon junket, it's the fact that I've failed to bring a lake trout to the fly—something I've been longing to do ever since Mitch first told me about landing big trout on light gear and small flies. Part of my folly lies in planning, having given myself only one evening to tackle the rich, laker-filled shoals of Tarfu Lake, and at a time when the lake decides to live up to its unpromising moniker.

It seems the same ghosts that haunted Lubbock are now bewitching Tarfu's fish, which splash merrily as we pout. The bewilderment is palpable among us. Instead of leaning back against hefty fish, we spend the night with our noses in our fly boxes, second-guessing our choices at every turn. By the time we pack

A colourful lake trout taken on a fly on Tarfu Lake.

up, everything from bushy streamers to minuscule emerger patterns have seen the lonely end of my line.

Allen Ginsberg once wrote of "redemption from wilderness." While I'm sure the hallucinatory beat poet wasn't writing about rebounding after getting skunked, I still find comfort in the concept. (And if anyone has heard ghosts in the trees, it's Ginsberg.) Redemption indeed arrives on the final hour of the last day of my trip, back on the azure waters of Atlin Lake. A sunny, calm day is just the omen I need, as I wade from one cluster of boulders to another, far from shore. I peel my waders to my waist, letting the sun scorch away the last remnants of bug repellent.

Atlin's aquatic residents, as if on retainer with the Yukon tourist board, are eager to send me home happy. And even though I had already caught many grayling on the trip, these treasures now emerging from the rocks—gleaming purple, blue, and gold in their own watery display of the northern lights—seem like a species all their own. In short order, I catch my tenth grayling in the same place with the same fly. As I lean down to release the fish and snip the slightly tattered Bead Head Pheasant Tail from my line, I realize this place that haunted me since childhood will continue to do so for the rest of my life.

Ghosts or not.

GRIZZLY CREEK LODGE, YUKON

by **Duane S. Radford**

> This article is dedicated to the memory of the late Doug Skanse of Bloomington, Minnesota, who had a vision for a lodge on the Lower Toobally Lake, Yukon. With the love and decorative talents of his wife Carol, Doug saw his dream finally come true in 2010. Credit is also extended to the present lodge owners David O'Farrell and his wife Reggie, along with their family, who helped Doug and Carol achieve their goal. If the Tree River Lodge, Nunavut, is one of the most remote lodges in Canada, then the Grizzly Creek Lodge on the Lower Toobally Lake, Yukon, must be a close second—it's that isolated. This is hands down one of the best locations anywhere for a lake trout fly-fishing adventure, and the fishing for grayling and pike is also great. For sheer beauty, the Upper Toobally Lake is in a class of its own; it's one of the most picturesque and enchanted places in Canada.

It's not every day that you're first at something, but my wife Adrienne and I enjoyed the distinction in 2010 of being the first-ever paying customers at Grizzly Creek Lodge on the Lower and Upper Toobally lakes in the Yukon wilderness, east of Watson Lake. After being under construction for more than a decade, the lodge finally opened its doors to the public, making my quest to visit the area possible. As it turned out, we were also the first people to ever fly-fish in the Upper Toobally Lake, which is connected to the Lower Toobally by the tortuous Smith River, navigable only by jet boat.

**One of northern Canada's most scenic spots.
Upper Toobally Lake, Grizzly Creek Lodge, Yukon.**

Noted American fly fisherman and author A.K. Best wrote, "It was the quest, not the prize" that created the dream of catching trout, and with it everything that brought him enjoyment. My quest to visit the Toobally lakes began when the late Yukon fisheries biologist Susan Thompson told me about the time she spent in this singularly outstanding area, describing it as a veritable Shangri-La. Susan had spent a couple of decades travelling the wilds of Yukon as a field biologist; consequently, I took her opinion as quite a testament. Starry eyed, she talked about the serenity of the area, the abundance of wildlife—especially the innumerable moose and majestic Trumpeter swans—and of course the great fishing for lake trout, pike, and Arctic grayling. It almost sounded like a religious experience the way Susan talked.

Log cabin at Grizzly Creek Lodge, Yukon.

The lodge was formerly owned by the late Doug Skanse of Bloomington, Minnesota, who sold it to David O'Farrell of Tagish, Yukon (a town located about 60 miles [97 km] south of Whitehorse), in 2013. Doug told me they started from scratch with just a few little cabins back in 1991 after buying Grizzly Creek Lodge in 1990. His first trip there was in 1983, one of many annual trips he made with one of his five children into various fishing lodges in the Canadian wilderness. In 1989, he decided that of all the places they'd travelled, Grizzly Creek Lodge topped the best in qualities he'd experienced. The former lodge owner's wife actually asked Doug if he wanted to buy the lodge during a later trip in 1990, and David O'Farrell subsequently popped the same question while guiding him on the water. Doug was a bit flustered and quer-

Dining room at Grizzly Creek Lodge, Yukon.

ied how he'd operate a lodge from his faraway home in Minnesota, to which Dave replied, "Well, that's why you hire a guy like me!"

Doug and his wife Carol are about as nice a couple as you'll ever meet, and they didn't want the lodge run like a convention centre, but rather as a very personal experience where guests were not just another number, so to speak. As unpretentious and caring people whose goal was to provide a little bit of heaven on earth for the itinerant fisher in the wilds of the Yukon, they set out to capitalize on the serenity of the surroundings—the main reason Doug bought the lodge (he was afraid somebody else would buy it and perhaps destroy its fine fishing and the true wilderness experience). Not to worry—with Carol's interior decorating talent adding to the ambience of the dining rooms and log cabins, anglers not only have a warm and welcoming environment, but they basically have the lakes to themselves during their stay. What's more, Doug takes comfort in knowing that David and his wife Reggie run the place the way he envisioned—not to mention Reggie's cooking will have you coming back for seconds.

David began working on building the lodge infrastructure with Doug in 1991, initially serving as a guide after having worked in that capacity for the former lodge owner. Very much at home in the wilderness, David—when not managing the lodge during the tourist season—guides big game hunters in the autumn and runs a trap line in the winter. He's your all-Canadian outdoorsman—a member of the Outdoor Writers of Canada and even a published author.

A trip to Grizzly Creek Lodge starts in Whitehorse, Yukon, the staging area for the Klondike gold rush in 1897. As part of the lodge package, we were booked into the upscale Skky boutique hotel beside the Alaska Highway, right across the road from the airport in Whitehorse. The lodge provided a rental car at no cost, and the next day we drove south to Watson Lake. Here we met up with Bill Seely of Northern Rockies Air for a flight in his de Havilland beaver, into the Lower Toobally Lake where the main lodge is located. After packing our gear aboard the floatplane, we were joined by two other guests—Americans Rob Zimmerman and Steven Andreae—at the base near Watson Lake for the flight into the lodge, which opens during the first week in June and operates until the end of August.

As the goal of the lodge manager is to maximize the quality of the trip with a focus on one-on-one customer service, they book only four guests per stay, so you'll have no competition during your trip. Also, although they offer guests a list of gear they should bring, the lodge provides virtually all the fishing gear you may need if you don't have proper tackle.

The Toobally Lakes are located about 100 km (62 mi) east of Watson Lake in the heart of the virgin Yukon wilderness. The main lodge is on the Lower Toobally Lake and is an architectural masterpiece, and the satellite lodge on the Upper Toobally Lake is situated on a picturesque point in one of the most splendid areas of the Yukon. With stand-alone characteristics that make them ideal for fly fishers, in particular, the lakes feature a number of large reefs, which act like magnets for lake trout and facilitate fly fishing in shallow water. While I seldom get all teary-eyed, I don't think I've ever been to a more charming spot than the lodge on the Upper Toobally Lake. Yes, Susan Thompson's captivating description of the area was dead on. The Toobally Lakes are truly outstanding in many ways.

With top-notch fishing for lake trout (both "chromers" and "red-fins") in shallow water, numerous northern pike as a bonus, plus trophy-class Arctic grayling a plenty—all on a fly rod—it doesn't get any better. In fact, it's the only such place I've been to in the Yukon, Northwest Territories, and Nunavut where the itinerant fly fisher can easily catch all three species at the same lodge. As if enjoying six "doubles" on lake trout and numerous pike and grayling wasn't enough, Adrienne and I were surrounded by scenery that is second to none in this area of secluded Yukon wilderness.

It may go without saying that the main attraction at Grizzly Creek Lodge is the fishing, which keeps getting better each year according to Doug Skanse and David O'Farrell. Let's face it, over the past 20 years the lodge has had virtually no fishing pressure; consequently, the fish stocks are in top shape. Doug says, "Those are my babies out there!" and is a strong advocate of catch-and-release fishing, with minimal handling. Yes, you'll enjoy a shore lunch or two of either Arctic grayling or a small lake trout while at the lodge, but all the trophy trout are returned to the water.

Duane Radford with a Grizzly Creek Lodge lake trout.

And when you return from your day on the lake, you'll feel right at home in your cozy cabin that features charming, rustic interior decor—chandeliers made of antlers, comfortable beds, wood-burning stoves, and plenty of space, topped off with shower rooms in each lodge that have hot and cold running water. You'll have quickly gotten to know the colourful staff on a personal basis, and you'll feel like you're in a first-class hotel.

As the owners have ensured, you're not just another number at Grizzly Creek Lodge. The opposite of an impersonal fish camp, it's not at all regimented, and whatever customers want to do is really up to them—including going out fishing until midnight (or even later) by themselves after dinner if that's their fancy in The Land of the Midnight Sun.

The Last Frontier: Tincup Wilderness Lodge, Yukon

by Duane S. Radford

> I don't think it's possible to find a more beautiful location for a remote fly-in fishing lodge than at Tincup Lake in the Yukon wilderness, which is situated some 250 km (155 mi) north of Whitehorse. I've visited the lodge three times while it was under the ownership of Larry Nagy and José Janssen, and it will always hold a special place in my heart. It is now under new ownership and has been extensively renovated, so I'm guessing it's even more enchanting than before. The lodge is located in a veritable Shangri-La, with breathtaking vistas of Tincup Lake and Ruby Mountain Range. It is one of Canada's most high-end adventure lodges and offers a plethora of amenities with excellent fishing for grayling, lake trout, pike, and seasonally, Chinook salmon.

Not exactly on the edge of the earth, but pretty close to it, Tincup Lake is located in Kluane Country in the Yukon, east of Mile 1,118 on the Alaska Highway. The area around Tincup Wilderness Lodge, which is situated on the shore of the lake, is untouched and one of the most enchanting spots North of Sixty in Canada. After having the pleasure of visiting this lodge three times, I'd go back again in a heartbeat.

Originally built by Ray Conant in 1969, burned down, and rebuilt by Larry Nagy in 1986, Tincup Wilderness Lodge has a long and eventful history. After the rebuild, Larry and his spouse José Janssen —the affable head chef renowned throughout the North Country for her exotic culinary talents—operated it until 2009. Then, in 2010, Meinrad Humm of Switzerland acquired the lodge. It was closed for renovations after Meinrad purchased it, then opened for business again in 2012.

Located in the verdant Ruby Range north of Kluane Lake— the largest lake in the Yukon—and internationally renowned Kluane National Park, Tincup Lake is one of the prettiest places I have been to North of Sixty. The landforms in the area are stunning: placid waters, towering peaks; and formidable, braided channels of the silty Kluane River to the west. One of the most spectacular places on earth, Kluane National Park is a truly majestic wilderness area, where I've seen as many as six grizzly bears while having a back country lunch. With an estimated 6,000–7,000 grizzlies in the Yukon, you definitely must be bear alert at all times. In fact, while fly fishing once for Arctic grayling in Tincup Creek at the outlet of the lake, the hair rose on the back of my neck, and I could sense the presence of something nearby. When I made my way downstream along the Tutchone First Nations trail beside the creek, I saw steaming grizzly bear scats— a grizzly had probably forded the creek just before I arrived!

Sifton Air glacier flight over Kluane National Park, Yukon.

For the fishing alone, I'd love to return to Tincup Lake—if only to even the score with Inconnu on nearby Kluane Lake. The lodge used to have fly-outs from Tincup Lake to catch both these monster predatory whitefish and northern pike; trouble is the Inconnu are a bit migratory and don't always stay in the same place (fishing for Inconnu is supposed to be best after mid-July). The lodge does, however, do fly-outs to nearby Dogpack Lake, where the lake trout and Arctic grayling seem to be stacked on top of each other—I don't think I've ever seen so many Arctic grayling in a lake North of Sixty!

After visiting Dogpack Lake with Larry Nagy, I can't say enough about the surreal feeling I had during my trip. If you want to share the feelings that Klondikers likely experienced in the wilds of the Yukon Territory during the gold rush, Dogpack Lake has it all.

There are many fine streams in northern Canada. Tincup Creek, Yukon.

Tincup Lake, and its outlet stream, Tincup Creek, both have exceptional trophy Arctic grayling fishing, not to mention the lake has a long history of some great fishing for lake trout, one of my favourite fish. Both Arctic grayling and lake trout are akin to wolves and grizzly bears—generally, you only find them in the wilderness. But while grayling are usually too precious for me to consider eating—tasty as they are—I don't mind a good feed of lake trout, and having a meal or two at the lodge is always a treat.

If you visit in late August, there's a run of King Salmon in Tincup Creek, while northern pike abound in a couple of lakes a short hike from Tincup Lake, proving that there's a lot of variety fishing-wise if that's what you're after.

When you aren't fishing, there are many other things to do at Tincup Wilderness Lodge—nature appreciation, wildlife viewing, hiking, photography, canoeing, and kayaking. An abundance of wildlife lives in the area: moose, Woodland caribou, Dall sheep, grizzlies and black bears, common and Arctic loons, Bald eagles—all true symbols of wilderness; and wildflowers in a profusion of hedysarum (wild sweet-vetch), mountain monkshood, prickly rose, fireweed, and asters pepper the alpine meadows near the lodge. If you're in the mood to relax, you can take a dip in the hot tub or spend some time in the sauna while taking in the scenery or reading a book. Afterward, you'll be treated to some of the finest cuisine at the lodge, likely with an international twist.

The lodge, open from mid-June to mid-September, offers 4- and 7-day packages from Whitehorse, Yukon, which includes return transportation between Whitehorse and the lodge, delicious home-cooked meals, and accommodations at the lodge. The cedar-log cabins feature two single beds; a private bathroom with hot and cold running water; shower, sink, and toilet; wood-burning stove; and electrical power supplied by a generator during daylight hours (18 hours a day in June, 19 hours in July, and 17 hours in August). In addition, the lodge provides aluminum boats with 15-horsepower motors—some with fish finders, fishing gear if you need it, and floater jackets/life vests.

With several ways to travel there, you'll have your pick of options. Air North has flights from Calgary and Edmonton in Alberta, Canada, and Vancouver, British Columbia, to Whitehorse from June 1–September 16, or you can drive the famed Alaska Highway if you prefer. Air Canada and West Jet also fly into Whitehorse from Vancouver, British Columbia, Canada, and Calgary/Edmonton, Alberta, Canada.

Guests departing for a day of fishing at Tincup Lake.

In preparation for fishing, drop in to Sports North in Whitehorse to buy your fishing licence and to gear up on your tackle—with its extensive, eclectic selection, it's a store that anglers dream about. Tincup Lake is cold and deep—it drops off to 600 feet just offshore in places, and you'll often find 200+ feet of water near the shoreline. It's ideal for jigging for lake trout, as well as trolling hardware or fly fishing for cruising lakers in the shallows during the early season. While some very large lake trout were taken from Tincup Lake when the lodge first opened, the largest I've seen on my trips were in the 25-pound range. Arctic grayling can be fished at various locations around the shoreline with fly-fishing or spin-fishing tackle, and some of the grayling are huge, in the 20-inch range. Tincup Creek also harbours many grayling all too eager to rise to a fly.

Apart from the fishing, you'll also want to take some time to explore Whitehorse: must-do tourist attractions are the Frantic Follies, a hilarious Klondike-era vaudeville performance in the Westmark Hotel; the Beringia Centre, an interpretive presentation of Yukon's fossil past on the Alaska Highway; the McBride Museum, with local artifacts and displays related to the gold rush; and the S.S. Klondike National Historic Site. Shopping and dining in Whitehorse is on par with major centres in Canada, if not better, and this modern city is well known for its thriving arts community. For first-rate accommodations, I recommend the High Country Inn, and I also encourage you to make one more side trip —many would say you haven't seen the Yukon until you've toured Dawson City, a four-hour drive north of Whitehorse, along the scenic Klondike Highway.

CHAPTER 8 | YUKON

Tincup Lake is billed as the "ultimate getaway" and for good reason—as former lodge owner Larry Nagy was fond of saying, "If you can't relax here, there's no hope for you!"

> Fishing licences for Canadian residents are very inexpensive in the Yukon:
>
> For Canadians: $15 (season) and $10 (6 days)
>
> For Non-Residents (U.S. & Overseas): $35 (season); $20 (6 days); and $10 (1 day)
>
> E-MAIL: info@tincup-lodge.com
>
> WEBSITE: www.tincup-lodge.com
>
> SATELLITE PHONE (from mid-June to mid-September): @1-604-484-4418
>
> PHONE: (in Switzerland) 41 43 455 0101

Chet Krygier (L) & Duane Radford with a northern pike from Kluane Lake.

Duane Radford with an Arctic grayling, Tincup Lake.

— 191 —

WELLESLEY LAKE: LAKE TROUT FLIES & FLY-FISHING TECHNIQUES

by Duane S. Radford

Wellesley Lake is located about 320 km (200 mi) northwest of Whitehorse. It's one of the Yukon's premier fisheries for lake trout and also features outstanding fishing for northern pike. Memories of my trip to Wellesley Lake will always be special because this is where I caught my largest-ever lake trout on a fly rod—a 35-pound trout on a purple Woolly Bugger streamer hand tied by my son, Myles—while fishing with Chuck Anderson of Kamloops, British Columbia. It went down as one of the all-time most exhilarating landings I've ever experienced, as the wind whipped the top off whitecaps while Chuck expertly navigated the outboard boat in Moose Bay.

When the first lake trout slammed into my streamer, my thoughts were still on a wonderful shore lunch cooked up by our affable chef, Jutta Senkowski. She's a great cook and I went back for seconds, thirds—it was almost embarrassing, the lunch was that good. Tasty fillets of pike and trout cooked to perfection; coleslaw and baked beans; potato salad and dinner rolls; dessert and hot beverages. It took the slam of a fish to rouse me from my food-induced bliss.

It was my first day on Wellesley Lake and my companion for the afternoon, Charles (Chuck) Anderson of Kamloops, British Columbia, Canada, and I had barely wet our lines when the 28-inch fish hit—not bad for starters on one of the North Country's premier lakes for trophy lake trout at Kluane Wilderness Lodge in Canada's Yukon Territory.

Chuck and I were fly fishing for lake trout in Moose Bay—in the southwest part of Wellesley Lake—having been blown off the main lake proper by a stiff wind from the south. There was no way we could sight cast on the legendary reef that skirted the north shore this afternoon, although it was pleasant enough otherwise, with temperatures in the 20°C range and overcast skies.

We had a couple of options: we could try our luck with blind casts or drift in the wind and troll. There was too much chop to cast safely, so drift it was. Before we rigged up, I checked the surface temperature—12°C, a couple of degrees above the preferred water temperature of 10°C for lake trout, so we'd have to fish deep to have any luck. Depths in Moose Bay are in the order of 20–30 feet, and for some reason, 24 feet was to be the jackpot on this spring day in June, dynamite for action.

Duane Radford with a Wellesley Lake, Yukon, lake trout.

After enticing that first 28-incher using a Conehead Purple Woolly Bugger (with rubber legs) that the lake trout just couldn't resist, I was feeling pretty good about the way things were going when another fish struck—this time a 24-inch broad-shouldered beauty, loaded with the rod-breaking, brutish strength so characteristic of lake trout. Then, just after coffee break, I thought I felt another strike—or was it?

To get any action when you're fishing for lake trout in midday, you normally have to fish deep, even in the spring when they're found in the shallows, because they're photophobic and bottom scavengers. Because of this, you can't always be sure of a strike; there's always a chance you may have snagged the bottom.

By this time, Chuck had switched to the same red-hot fly I was using and was similarly enjoying frequent takes. I casually mentioned to him that I might have a hookup but wasn't absolutely sure. Because lake trout have tough jaws, I ripped the fly line to make sure I had a solid hook set.

Before long, I could sense the movement of a big fish and I told Chuck I might have hit pay dirt. I'd lost too many trophy fish over the years to take things lightly in such instances, and I'd have to focus hard to make sure I landed this fish. It's at times like this that a knowledgeable fishing partner is a blessing, and as I took in slack line and brought the fish to reel, Chuck reeled in his line and raised the outboard motor, an expectant look in his eye.

This fish was intent on having his own way and wouldn't budge, which is typical behaviour for a big lake trout (you know how stubborn a mule can be—ditto for lake trout of any size). It was like being hooked to a cement truck with the emergency brake on tight. In these situations, you have to let some line out, pump the rod, and hope the fish will move (a bit). If things look really bad, it's also a good idea to ask your partner to start the motor and cover the distance between you and the fish to give you better leverage, if the boat's drifting in the wind.

It wasn't long before I sent out the SOS to Chuck and he fired up the motor, maneuvering the boat in the direction of the fish. There was simply too much pressure on the rod and line for them to stand up against both the force of the wind drift and size of the fish. Something would have to give. A closing tactic was essential if I was to have any chance of landing this behemoth with a fly rod.

Once you get a large trout going, you can use the flex in the rod, as well as the drag of the reel, and stretch in the line to start the long, slow process of bringing it to the surface—tiring it out as the trout struggles to keep its position. As Chuck bought me some time, sure enough, I started to feel the trout yield and rise towards the surface.

After a few more minutes, I caught sight of the fish, and then I really got excited. What a monster! When it saw the boat, it turned and sounded; there was no way to stop it. Line screeched from my reel and all I could do was palm the spool, keeping the rod at arm's length. It must have run for at least 75 yards before it stopped, well into my backing. And so it went for the next half hour as I slowly brought it in, only to have it make yet another run. My wrist was starting to ache and the biceps in my right arm were pained, but I kept pressure on the fish, never giving any more ground than necessary, continuing to pump the rod and take in line, inch by inch. Yes, thoughts of knots yielding did come to mind while I worried that the trout would throw the hook when it charged the boat—creating slack line, which is always a danger—but I persevered nonetheless.

Finally, when I was confident the fish was sufficiently winded, I asked Chuck to help land it in our fish cradle as I drew it towards the boat. I could have kissed him as he expertly slid the cradle under the trout and lifted it out of the water. For the first time—in what seemed like an eternity—my heart started to beat again, and I breathed a huge sigh of relief as I watched him gently lay the fish on the floor of the boat. Just as suddenly, the hook dropped from its jaw—I was that close to losing it!

My baby weighed 35 pounds (estimated by Don Toews, then Yukon Fisheries Director) and Chuck taped it at 32" fork length (36" total length). After a few photos, I lowered it into the water, then watched it revive and swim to the murky depths of Moose Bay. During that afternoon, I caught six fine lake trout, all on the Conehead Purple Woolly Bugger—the smallest being 22 inches. *Oh, what a party!*

LAKE TROUT FACTS

Lake trout taken with a streamer.

A member of the "char" family, lake trout are creatures of cold water and generally reside in deep, unproductive lakes. When surface waters warm during the summer, they will migrate to the hypolimnion, below the thermocline, to find preferred temperatures in the depths of a lake. During the spring and autumn, they will be spread throughout a lake when the temperatures are homothermous, and they spawn over submerged reefs in the autumn.

The bloodhounds of still waters, with keen olfactory senses able to detect subtle movements in the water, they feed on all manner of forage fish, preferring Cisco (also called Tullibee) or lake whitefish, where these species are present. Known to be cannibalistic, they can reach enormous sizes, the largest being a 102-pound giant caught in commercial gill nets in Lake Athabasca, which straddles the Alberta/Saskatchewan border. In parts of northern Canada, it is not uncommon to catch lake trout over 50 pounds, either on spinning tackle or using jigs.

You can sight-cast to lake trout as they cruise the shallows during the spring and autumn, or take your luck with blind casts using a sink-tip or floating line if you see them breaching the surface but can't actually see them underwater. Trolling (slowly) can also be effective at these times of the year, using a full-sink or sink-tip line, and if they're in deeper water, you can catch them trolling by doing "figure eights," ripping the line from time to time and then letting it drop. Using the wind drift is often highly effective—on lakes where submerged reefs are present, station yourself in knee-deep water and sight-cast to lake trout as they skirt the reef. Also try fishing dropoffs along the shoreline by pitching a streamer as far out as possible and letting it sink to the bottom—it's not uncommon for a lake trout to strike as you begin your retrieve. Because they live in an impoverished environment, they tend to eat whatever comes their way.

All sorts of streamers will catch lake trout, and I've taken them on many different patterns. For starters, however, I suggest you try the following best bets: Bunny Strip Leach, Conehead Woolly Bugger, Olive Matuka, and Tincup Special.

As they're THE "big game" fish of the freshwater aquatic ecosystem in North America, fly fishing for lake trout is very challenging because of their brute strength and enormous size, but it is one of the most rewarding experiences I've ever had.

In case you're wondering how can you shorten the learning curve for fly fishing for lake trout, I offer the following pointers:

- ❖ Use a full-sink line with a short leader when the fish are deep.
- ❖ Make absolutely certain your hooks are razor sharp, and set the hook with an attitude or they'll throw the fly.
- ❖ Use a #8- or 9-weight rod, matching line, 2X or larger leader, with at least 100 yards of backing, preferably 150–200 yards.
- ❖ Check the water temperature—they prefer 10°C.
- ❖ Fish as close to the bottom as possible during midday; target inshore areas during the evening and early morning.
- ❖ Work prime lairs, patiently and systematically, as they're not everywhere.
- ❖ Keep the tension on, if you do hook a trout, until you land it.
- ❖ Fish accordingly for a top predator, as lake trout tend to come on as light intensity drops in the late afternoon and evening.

STREAMER PATTERNS FOR LAKE TROUT

Bunny Strip Leach

Hook: Curved, short shank, size 2–6

Thread: Black 6/0

Body: Chenille or peacock

Wing: Rabbit fur cut in 3/16" strip. Wrap thread from the eye back to just above the hook point. Measure a length of rabbit strip about 1 1/2 the length of the hook shank, with the natural lay of the fur pointing back. Tie the strip on with several wraps; next, wrap the thread to the hook eye. Finally, wrap the fur forward around the shank and tie off. Trim off excess fur at the eye and finish with a well-formed thread wrap. Whip finish and glue.

Head: Bead (medium/large lead) or cone, optional

Comments: Attractor pattern. Imitates baitfish; large leach.

Conehead Woolly Bugger

Hook: Long shank, size 2–8

Thread: To match body 6/0

Tail: Black marabou, with 4–5 strands of pearl Krystal flash

Body: Purple chenille

Head: Cone

Comments: Try this pattern in purple, olive, black, or brown. Add rubber legs on thorax. Imitates large leech or baitfish.

Olive Matuka

Hook: Long streamer, size 4–10

Thread: Olive, 6/0

Body: Olive chenille

Hackle: Olive hen neck

Wing: Olive hen or cock neck feathers

Rib: Gold tinsel, to hold down the wing

Comments: The Matuka-style streamer pattern originated in New Zealand for rainbow trout and imitates small baitfish. Other variations of this pattern can be tied to imitate caddis fly adults.

Tincup Special

Hook: Curved, short shank, size 4–6

Thread: Black, 3/0

Body: Pearl diamond braid

Wing: Blue over lime over white bucktail

Topping: Pearl Krystal flash

Eyes: Yellow audible eyes

Comments: Imitates small baitfish

YUKON'S TOP STREAM FOR 'BOWS, THE KATHLEEN RIVER

by **Duane S. Radford**

A fishing excursion for rainbow trout on the Kathleen River, Yukon, is a must-do for the itinerant angler—it's one of Canada's top streams for rainbow trout, with trophy Arctic grayling as a bonus, and lots of lake trout seasonally. A fly-fisherman's paradise, this large, freestone river is located south of Haines Junction about 150 km (95 mi) west of Whitehorse, capital of the Yukon. Haines Junction is the gateway to Kluane National Park, arguably one of the most spectacular regions in Canada.

The jagged peaks of the St. Elias Mountain Range stab the heavens as a backdrop to the charming Kathleen River. One of the few spots in the Yukon where 'bows occur naturally in northernmost Canada—a throwback to the last ice age when they likely became landed immigrants in this northern territory when water is thought to have flowed from Alaska into the Yukon some 12,000 years ago—the Kathleen also boasts some excellent fishing for Arctic grayling as well as lake trout (seasonally).

This rushing river flows out of Kathleen Lake in Kluane National Park, where breathtaking rainbows also reside. Even if you weren't there to fish for 'bows, Arctic grayling, and lake trout, a side trip to Kathleen Lake would be icing on the cake of any trip to the Yukon. The region around the lake and river is a land of primal beauty and home to numerous wildlife. In addition to black and grizzly bears, the area abounds with mountain goats, moose, all manner of birds of prey (bald eagles, osprey, kingfishers, and herons), and multiple waterfowl. The profusion of wildflowers along the lake shore and river banks make it all the more beautiful.

I've had the good fortune to have fly-fished the Kathleen River several times during the past decade, and every trip has been rewarding. I've now fished the river during the spring, summer, and autumn, delighting in using not only dry flies, but nymphs and streamers as well. Because of the variable flows during the spring runoff, it's best to pack not only a floating line, but also a sink-tip and full-sink fly line. And since you can't predict what the flows might be, it's best to come loaded for bear. Bear spray is a must, along with a flare gun loaded with bear bangers. "Yo bear, yo bear!" is a common call among anglers in the area.

* Note that a licence (one day or annual) is required to fish in Kluane National Park, whereas a Yukon Angling Licence is required outside of the park.

Yukon licence fees:
For Canadian Residents: $25 (season); $15 (6 days); $10 (1 day).
For Non-Residents: $35 (Season); $20 (6 days); $10 (1 day).

Kathleen River, Yukon, with St. Elias Mountain Range in background.

To capitalize on the best fishing in the Kathleen River, I recommend booking a guided jet boat trip out of the Dalton Trail Lodge (867-634-2099; info@daltontrail.com; www.daltontrail.com), which is located south of Haines Junction along the Haines Highway. The lodge is situated on Dezadeash Lake, a large lake well known for excellent angling for lake trout, in particular (there's also terrific fishing for northern pike at the outlet, locally known as Six Mile). I've stayed at the lodge many times, and it's one of my favourite North Country destinations, with exquisite dining and fine accommodations. The owners—Hardy and Trix Ruf, Jacqueline and Mike MacCannell, and Shelly and Robert Shaw—are great hosts and have top-notch fishing guides. What's more, the *National Geographic Traveler Magazine* granted three stars to the Dalton Trail Lodge, the highest designation awarded by the publication.

Experts on the whereabouts of fish throughout the season, the guides here are truly impressive. For one example, when I wanted to catch a lake trout appetizer on one of my many trips to the Kathleen River with my wife Adrienne, former lodge part-owner and guide Thomas Staub recommended a certain pool, and you guessed it—we caught our appetizer just like that. On another trip with local guide Dan Drummond, he put us on a lake trout hotspot where we caught our fish appetizer when we didn't expect to late in the day. And after you catch that appetizer? The chef at the lodge will prepare it as a treat before your four-course dinner, provided you get back to the lodge before 6:00 p.m.

If walk-and-wade fishing is your fancy, you can enjoy it on the Kathleen River in the vicinity of the Haines highway bridge crossing, downstream a short distance to the Lower Kathleen Lake, locally known as Mud Lake. Because it's a large river, too deep to ford in most places, it can only be fished effectively with a jet boat (most often, jet boats are used to access remote areas that would be otherwise inaccessible for walk-and-wade anglers, although there are spots where trolling is productive). Impassable falls in the lower reaches of the Kathleen River make the river treacherous even for a jet boat, however, so I don't recommend a downstream trip without a competent fishing guide.

> Only single-pointed barbless hooks are permitted by law on the Kathleen River. The daily limit for lake trout is one; all lake trout longer than 65 cm must be released. The daily limit for Arctic grayling is two; all longer than 40 cm must be released. All rainbow trout, regardless of size, must be released.

When it comes to fishing for 'bows, they can be taken on all manner of fly patterns: attractor flies, Bead Head nymphs, and streamers. I normally follow the same drill I would anywhere, but it's a good idea to bring an arsenal of flies because changeups are often required. I'll start by using attractor patterns, such as the Turks Tarantula, Madame X, Chernobyl Ant, and different coloured Stimulators; Elk-hair caddis and Grey Wulff dries are also old standbys. All of these are generally producers, but if the bite slows down, I'll switch to Woolly Buggers, particularly Coneheads, especially if I'm targeting 'bows, lake trout, or grayling while sight casting. Spin casters favour Mepps spinners and small spoons.

As the Kathleen River is crystal clear, it's possible to see rainbow trout and lake trout in shallow water. If the fish won't rise to a dry fly, I'll usually switch to a streamer; Bead Head nymphs are also producers if the rise slows down. Casting is usually a dream on the Kathleen River except in places up tight against the bank, where snags on willows might be an issue and roll casts become the norm.

Myles Radford with a rainbow trout, Kathleen River, Yukon.

> Stay a while and make a booking for a First Nations cultural and historical interpretation and wildlife viewing tour on Kathleen Lake with Ron Chambers (867-634-2378) of Kruda Che Boat Tours (www.krudache.com) to enjoy the majesty of Kluane National Park from the comfort of a large cabin cruiser. Expect to see both black and grizzly bears from the safety of a tour boat amid the snow-capped peaks of Canada's Himalayas—the Saint Elias Mountain Range. While you're in the area, also book a "flight-seeing" trip over some of the world's largest glaciers in Kluane National Park with Sifton Air in Haines Junction (867-634-2916) for an exhilarating sightseeing experience over the world's largest inland ice field. For more information: email siftonair@northwestel.net

Kruda Che Boat Tours – Kathleen Lake, Kluane National Park, Yukon.

A fishing trip to the Yukon would be incomplete without spending some time on the Kathleen River. While you're vacationing in the Yukon, make the most of your trip by taking a glacier sightseeing trip and some Kluane Country side trips on the Kathleen Lake. The Kathleen is truly one of those quintessential streams that should be on the bucket list of every angler.

IF YOU GO: Check out the Yukon Tourism & Culture (www.tc.gov.yk.ca) and Yukon Larger Than Life (www.travelyukon.com) websites for information on things to do in the Yukon, how to get there, and accommodations. There are flights into Whitehorse from Calgary/Edmonton and Vancouver that are available on Air Canada, Air North, and West Jet. Make a vacation of your trip, and stay awhile to see the sights.

CHAPTER 8 | YUKON

Yukon's Unique Fishing Lodge: Dalton Trail Lodge

by Duane S. Radford

> The Dalton Trail Lodge is a unique fishing lodge—in the heart of the Yukon, an area that's a fisherman's paradise—with outstanding accommodations and fine dining that features the widest variety of fishing opportunities anywhere North of Sixty. I have now visited this lodge six times, the same number of trips that co-editor Ross H. Shickler made to Plummer's Arctic Lodge on Great Bear Lake. Ross kept returning to Great Bear Lake because of the outstanding fishing—the same reason I keep going back to the Dalton Trail Lodge, which is like a second home to my family and me.

If you're interested in a one-stop fishing adventure in Yukon for several kinds of fish out of one lodge, look no further than the Dalton Trail Lodge (www.daltontrail.com) located near Kluane National Park, one of the world's most rugged and spectacular parks. The lodge is a couple of hours drive west of Whitehorse, and a short drive south of Haines Junction beside the road to Haines, Alaska.

Situated on the shore of Dezadeash Lake, a large lake on the flanks of the towering St. Elias Mountains—Canada's Himalayas—the Dalton Trail Lodge offers both day trips and overnighters to dozens of nearby lakes and streams. It's a convenient staging centre in the heart of the Yukon wilderness, and itinerant fishermen should be prepared for all manner of adventures.

Most of the time, clients travel to the local hotspots from the lodge by vehicle, but there are some trips that require quads or helicopters. If you don't want to leave the lodge, you can also fish in Dezadeash Lake right off the doorstep of your cozy cabin for both lake trout and Arctic grayling—or at Six Mile, at the lake's outlet, a quintessential pike fisherman's dream. For an adventure in itself, you can opt to access Six Mile by quad.

Side trips to Kathleen Lake in nearby Kluane National Park and to the Louise River for grayling should be top of list, as well as a wilderness adventure at Mush Lake for lake trout and at the lake's outlet stream for grayling too numerous to fathom. In addition to further fishing opportunities for lake trout, guests can enjoy nonstop action for Arctic grayling on several local streams, one of them within walking distance of the lodge.

Dalton Trail Lodge, Yukon.

Even after six trips to this fisherman's paradise, I have barely tapped all the fishing adventures available at the lodge—for varying species of fish—that can't be experienced at any other lodge in Yukon, or elsewhere in Canada for that matter. But I can claim that I've fished for lake trout, Arctic grayling, Dolly Varden, northern pike, and rainbow trout—all in one stay—and caught all of these species, despite having cold spells with strong, steady winds on some trips, which are not unusual in the mountains.

For an exhilarating experience if there ever was one, a jet boat trip on the Kathleen River is a must-do excursion for a visiting fisherman. Then there's nearby Stella Lake, a short hike off the highway to Haines, Alaska, where I had a brush with a grizzly bear and delighted in fishing for abundant Dolly Varden—which will take a great variety of lures and are not hard to catch—and watching the antics of some resident bald eagles. I've also enjoyed many days fishing on the Kathleen River, arguably one of the greatest fly-fishing rivers in Canada, in search of its legendary rainbow trout (one of the few places in Yukon where rainbows are present).

Jet boat fly fishing on the Kathleen River, Yukon.

For the street-smart fisherman, there are lots of places to fish without a (lodge) guide that are within a couple of hours drive, at most. You really don't need a guide for most trips if you have any amount of bush savvy, but there are many places where one is definitely recommended. I'd suggest booking at least two or three guided day trips to get off on the right foot and make the most of your vacation while at the lodge. And as a note of caution, grizzly bears and black bears are not uncommon along the Haines highway in this area, so you'll want to be prepared if you encounter one.

Air North flies out of Calgary, Edmonton, and Vancouver into Whitehorse, while Air Canada flies out of Vancouver into Whitehorse—the jumping-off point for the Dalton Trail Lodge. The lodge will make arrangements to pick you up at Whitehorse and drop you off at the airport for your return flight, or you can rent a vehicle in Whitehorse and travel on your own to and from the lodge. Rental cars are likewise available at the lodge. You can take also take the Alaska Highway from Edmonton to Whitehorse (2,070 km) if you would rather drive—on a paved road—than fly. Incidentally, the food at the lodge is excellent!

**(below)
Enormous pike can be taken out
of the Dalton Trail Lodge.
(supplied)**

**(above)
Happy anglers with a lake trout
from Dezadeash Lake. (supplied)**

CHAPTER 9

A Woman's Perspective of North of Sixty
by **Adrienne E. Radford**

> Adrienne Radford is the wife of co-editor Duane S. Radford and lives in Edmonton, Alberta. Born and raised in Calgary, Alberta, she's been an outdoor girl since she was a child and was a Girl Guide leader for many years. Adrienne is the Awards Chair for the Outdoor Writers of Canada and has accompanied her husband on numerous fishing trips throughout Canada, where she's honed her skills as a fly fisher. Her trips have included fishing for Atlantic salmon on the Miramichi River (New Brunswick), Coho salmon out of Campbell River (British Columbia), and Chinook salmon on Lake Ontario, as well as various fishing in the Kenauk Reserve (Quebec), the Grand River (Ontario), Wapata Lake and the Cree River (Saskatchewan), Cornwall and Wylie lakes (Alberta), Dezadeash Lake, Grizzly Lake Lodge, Mush Lake, and Tincup Lake (Yukon), and Great Bear Lake (NWT).

North of Sixty: that's where I've had the best fishing adventures, which began in my childhood a long time ago. A lot has changed over the years.

I was born and raised in Calgary, Alberta, Canada, as a city girl, but my parents loved the outdoors and adventure. As a result, my sister, Lucille, and I were exposed at a very early age to the pleasures, challenges, and cautions of fishing. Armed with huge, awkward rods and spinning reels, we snagged underbrush along rivers, pulled logs to shore in numerous lakes, and survived many drowning opportunities as we travelled all across Canada. Sometimes we even caught fish! The possibility of landing a fish was the impetus to embark on adventures over and over again. As we became seasoned outdoor girls, Mom and Dad were quite willing to let us set up tents, cook over an open fire, and harangue them with our knowledge of the outdoors. After all, we were Girl Guides with lots of outdoors-related badges. Little did I realize that this was boot-camp training for a life of adventure all over Canada!

At university, I met a handsome science student. By 1969, he had become my husband, my best friend, and my new fishing buddy. This freshly minted fisheries biologist knew where to go fishing because he had done research on lakes in northern Alberta during the summer months, and so we were off to explore The North. The words *holiday* and *fishing* had always been synonymous for me, but "North of Sixty"? It was a new adventure and as the "adventure" level ramped up, there were often times when I wanted to tell my new husband where to go! But I persevered: I was young, in love, and soon fell in love with North of Sixty.

Our first foray, in 1972, was a lot different from fishing in the North today. We drove dreary miles in our 1968 Chevy Malibu from our home in Lethbridge in southern-most Alberta, to Fort McMurray in northern-most Alberta. I got the back seat along with all the gear that couldn't be crammed into the trunk. In those days you took it all, or did without. So we had tents, cooking equipment, food, sleeping bags, fishing gear, clothes, an axe, and a form of "protection" before all the rules on gun control in Canada—the list seemed endless. Did I mention that two 6-foot men had the whole front seat to themselves, bucket seats and all, or that in those days "highway" 63 was a glorified game trail? From Fort McMurray we flew, in progressively smaller planes, to Fort Chipewyan and then out to Wylie Lake, in the middle of nowhere just south of the 60th. But a week on that lake in the middle of nowhere had me hooked.

We were back again in 1974, this time to sample the bragging-size lake trout in Cornwall Lake, another lake in the Pre-Cambrian Shield in northern Alberta just south of the 60th parallel. On this trip, I was with three men in two trucks, a little wiser and more experienced, but in those days with still the same amount of—if not more—big, awkward gear. And don't believe for one minute that men take less stuff! Fisher-MEN need all sorts of options in equipment, tackle, line, lures, reels, and more for their fishing pleasure. They also need more food and beverages, but not necessarily many changes of clothes!

This time we flew from Edmonton to Fort McMurray, still a one-building, gravel-runway airport, then to Fort Chipewyan—then a dirt-strip landing in the wilderness—and crammed our gear and bodies into two floatplanes out to Cornwall Lake. The North of Sixty airports in those days were basic: strips of cleared land with a windsock. The planes got smaller and more rustic with every stop, and the communication between plane, pilot, and base got iffier. In fact, when it came time to leave Cornwall Lake, we packed up and waited ... and waited ... and wondered how we'd make our plane connections. We'd requested a "pick-up" no later than 9:00 a.m. to make connections back to the South, but without radios we couldn't "call up" our pilots to find out where they were. But at last, though it's very quiet in the North, we finally detected the sound of mechanization—only it was one plane when there should have been two. With limited air services in the North, one of our planes was needed elsewhere, so we all had to go out in one. Now, *we* were the "fish": sardines in a can. I didn't stand a chance in a crash because I was the smallest by far; I was also so far back in the tail I couldn't breathe, which didn't matter—I was holding my breath anyway, and praying. After a rather hard landing on a small lake near Fort Chip, all of us could have used some physiotherapy to unkink and resume normal feeling in our limbs. But, we were all breathing again.

Those were the days of real adventure. My husband and I shared a pup tent (when you're packing it in, you pick small accommodations and hope that you don't have any wildlife visitors), and we shivered in our own sleeping bags. In later years, they developed better fabrics, insulation with more resistance to cold, and bags that zipped together. Oh, yeah! Still, nobody prayed for good weather like I did.

**Accommodations then:
Tent camp at Cornwall Lake, Alberta.**

On those ultimate DIY adventures, we cooked out of doors, washed dishes and body parts in the lake (formed by glacial deposits and still about as cold), and looked after body functions off in the distance. Little had I imagined that I could eat fish breakfast, lunch, and dinner and still consider myself blessed. Refrigeration didn't happen and storage was a challenge, so the accoutrements to a meal were canned or freeze dried, and basic. There was always the concern for bulk and weight on the miniscule plane—back then, rods weren't collapsible, and warmth was synonymous with weight in clothing—so because the equipment we took was awkward, bulky, and weighty, you had to think out very carefully what you really needed, not wanted, to take. "Compact" doesn't describe the equipment of those years.

Adrienne Radford with a lake trout at Wylie Lake, Alberta.

On those lakes, I was introduced to experiences I'd never had before and fish like I'd never seen before: huge lake trout, walloping white fish, and ponderous pike. On one lake there was an antique boat that remained water worthy, but that meant hoping the motor would work and the fuel cache was intact when you arrived. On our first trip to Wylie Lake, we opted for inflatables, but that meant pumping it up for hours and hoping you never got caught in the wind. But the fantastic fishing made the "challenges" all worthwhile. Being the only woman on the trip, I tried hard to "be good," but I often thought I was going to "catch it" because I'd snagged, yet again, another log and would lose, yet again, another lure. But often to my surprise, after a lot of playing the line, I discovered that I was on the other end of a line with a big fish.

We were younger and slimmer, my husband had more hair, and we were probably foolish, but what memories we have of North of Sixty. Thank goodness no one became ill or injured way out there in the sticks. That's the way it was in those days.

So, what's changed North of Sixty? As I've grown older, the North has matured. In those days, fishing was an economy with small commercial outfits selling their fish to southern neighbours, or was a necessity, with trappers fishing to feed their dogs. Although these traditions linger to some extent and the ubiquitous poacher still exists, fishing is now predominantly recreational and associated with "doing business." Air charters, boat charters, and lodges are now the economies.

These days you will never be crammed into a plane; the aircraft charter companies are numerous and the planes more modern with constant communication available between their base and the lodges. You feel safe knowing someone is there if a need arises, and air and water craft operators give you a safety course before you begin your adventure. Furthermore, there's better communication and enforcement, so don't forget your licence.

One of the biggest changes is that the DIY rustic campsite has been replaced with WOW-factor fishing lodges. Forget the outdoor plumbing and bathing in glacial lakes; you'll have a plethora of amenities at the various lodges. In the Yukon, at the Dalton Trail Lodge on Dezadeash Lake—near the Kathleen River and Kathleen Lake—you can enjoy various styles of your own log cabin with a sitting area, separate bedrooms for members in your party, and bathrooms with flush toilet, shower, hot water, and lush towels. On my first trip to Dalton Trail, I was ill the first day we arrived, but in our cabin, I had more comforts than at home.

Accommodations now: Tincup Wilderness Lodge, Yukon.

I was attended to by the staff bringing my lunch, tea, and hot water bottles and asking what else they could get me. What a welcome change from toughing it out on a wind-swept lake in a tent—alone!

At Grizzly Creek Lodge, also in the Yukon, your cabin includes a wood-burning stove and only a short hike to the wash facilities, which are equipped better than any five-star hotel—even Martha Stewart would marvel at the décor. And though dinner is served with linens and wine glasses, there's no need to "dress"— you're supposed to come in your fishing duds. Remember, you're there to fish, so casual is the word and you're welcome to help yourself in the kitchen anytime. Because fishing North of Sixty used to be strictly a testosterone tie, your sleeping arrangements may still be a single bed, but look on the bright side—covers all to yourself and perhaps less snoring?

Besides being equipped with a canteen, fishing supplies, maybe a few souvenirs of the lodge, and a bar operated on the honour system, the main lodges are stocked with anything you might need to stay "in" on a bad-weather day: books, games, reference material, and local historical interest items. The main lodge at Plummer's Great Slave Lake camp has a fireplace and sitting area that encourages lots of fish tale swapping, which is typical of many lodges. Perusing the walls is an education, and Plummer's even has a daily "fibbers check-in," where the biggest fish caught that day is recorded. Personally, I'm not too concerned about how many and the biggest: I'm there for the fishing and the fun. Besides, since most fishermen stretch the truth anyway, you might choose to quietly avoid the competition. And speaking of the fishing, it's just as good as it was in the "old days" because the lodges look after the fish just as much as they look after you. They keep track of their fish in terms of "the take," the rate of catch, and the fish health to maintain their fishery resource.

Another perk is that no longer do you invariably have to sit on ant-infested, rotting logs; you'll have your own deck and enjoy a lakeside view of gorgeous scenery and tranquility. Our cabin deck at Tincup Wilderness Lodge in the heart of the Yukon, for example, included rockers and expansive scenery. If you want even more solitude, at Grizzly Creek you can make arrangements to go to Upper Toobolly Lake and have your own "all alone" stint at the lodge and cabins.

Despite all of the outdoor action you may partake in, it's important to know that none of these lodges will care about your Weight Watchers creed. Fantastic food is their motto; breakfast can be a bountiful buffet or a daily special request like those prepared by Red Seal chefs at the Cree River Lodge in Northern Saskatchewan (just south of the 60th parallel, but close enough to be North of Sixty). Suppers are never "repeats" or leftovers and include desserts as the crowning glory. Everything is homemade, and despite shipping costs, fruits and veggies are abundant on the table and available day long. No freeze-dried food in sight!

And shore lunch? During the day, all fish are catch and release, but the appropriate size is kept for lunch. There's nothing like catching your own and watching the guide set up lunch camp, cook, and clean up. Fish are prepared differently every day, and each guide has a specialty. A "light" lunch of beans and creamed corn from a can, potatoes fried over the fire, and huge cookies for dessert is accompanied by cold water, pop, or beer. Don't listen to your arteries; just eat, enjoy, and know it won't last. Shore lunches can also be an exploring adventure. While our guide was preparing lunch, I was discovering old trapper's cabins and an ice house on the Cree River, following game trails, spotting wildlife, and finding fossils on Great Slave Lake.

The guide provided by the lodge is your best friend; respect and acknowledge this resource as he is responsible for the success of your day. Besides preparing the boat, checking equipment, being your tour guide for the region, preparing your shore lunch, and keeping you safe and comfortable, he will be an expert on fish —where they are, what to use to catch them, and fishing technique. Being the woman on the trip, I have found it best to listen to the guide and learn. I don't get into a "who's the expert" contest with him. If you take his advice, show you're willing to try, and have a sense of humour, you can't go wrong.

After a knee replacement, I was quite apprehensive about trekking into the wilderness; on a fishing trip, who wants to babysit a woman, let alone a gimp? Knowing my condition, the guide on a later Dalton Trail Lodge trip was cautious with me— that is, until I slid on rocks and fell down in the river, laughing with relief that I'd survived my first fall and my fishing career wasn't over. From my perspective, my outdoor life wasn't compromised; that guide was there to catch me and just as relieved that I was game for more. The moral? Show 'em that women can be part of North of Sixty life.

And what's the hidden bonus? I believe it's because I listen to guides, want to learn, take instruction, and am willing to try everything that I usually end up out-fishing my husband—and he's an awesome fly fisherman. Between the two of us, I am typically rewarded with the biggest and/or the most!

David O'Farrell (L) and Adrienne Radford with a lake trout at Grizzly Creek Lodge, Yukon.

North of Sixty women have come a long way. They aren't the dance hall girls or rugged pioneers of yore, but rather the guides, support staff, and frequent co-owner/operator of lodges. In the past, sportsmen's shows were in their infancy, and participants were promoting trips to faraway places. Today, representatives from North of Sixty are the primary participants. At today's huge shows, you'll find many women "manning" the booths who are owners of the best lodges —a reflection of women's increasing role North of Sixty. But the "male territory" attitude can linger, so go with care and don't step on the testosterone. Have an open mind as every place is unique and offers a new and exciting experience. And know that you might have to overlook a few things—in this formerly man's world, you may still be a guest.

Another word of advice: Don't let those "South of Sixty-ers" tell you fishing is better on the coast for the "big ones." I've salmon-fished the Miramichi in New Brunswick and at Painter's Lodge in Campbell River, and it's just as exciting as landing Atlantic or Coho salmon. It is important, however, to know the type of fishing you want. Most lodges have access to both lake (boat and from shore) and river fishing, but will it be lure or fly?

My fishing career started with a spinning rod and reel with hardware lures, then moved to "upgraded" rods, reel, and lures, and now I'm a fly-fishing addict. It might not land the biggest fish, but it takes a lot of skill to land that fly where you want it, move it around, and set the hook at just the right time. Fly fishing offers tons of action and is a lot better than casting a lure and reeling it in—and you can easily adapt to a little trolling across the lake when you're off to a new location to fly-fish. Look at those outdoor magazine covers with fish leaping in the air, flashing sunlight and colours—you'll usually spot a fly fisher-person behind it with a big grin!

I've experienced a wide variety of fishing, with some of the best grayling fishing during evenings at Tincup Wilderness Lodge, listening to loons and boating into secluded inlet streams on the lake in the evening; and out of the Dalton Trail Lodge, where the Kathleen River offers an abundance of diverse grayling experiences. I would love to have my ashes spread along that river so I can swim with the fishes. As for pike fishing, Grizzly Creek Lodge and Cree River Lodge offer the likes of which I haven't seen since our first foray North of Sixty. There's nothing like a 40-incher on a fly at Cree River Lodge, and every lodge has had lake trout to die for.

If you're really getting into it, you'll want to start collecting your own equipment. Although the lodges will provide what you need, it's been well used; the new equipment is lighter, doesn't knick or break like it used to, and with your own tackle box, you don't have to give back that "hot" lure/fly. And don't worry if you don't have everything; remember, you're going to utilize that guide you're paying for and he'll have anything you need. But do take two of everything, including rods, because if one breaks, there goes your vacation—it'll be a long day for you in the boat watching the other fishermen.

Remember, fishing is a balm to the soul and a stimulus to the mind. You're always learning about types of fish, habits and habitats, lures and flies, and how to "read the water," and most anglers are willing to share their fishing philosophies.

Are you ready to venture North of Sixty yet? If the answer is yes, I recommend you do your research first so you'll be well prepared. The good news is that there are more options and easier access to North of Sixty now than ever before: more lodges, guides, and outfitters to enhance your experience; decreased cost (compare prices to an all-inclusive!); the convenience of lighter weight, less bulky, warmer equipment; and more amenities than in the "olden days." Consider what you're looking for in a fishing adventure—will you need runners, gum boats, and/or waders?— and explore the various locations to see what draws you.

Besides investigating lodges and lakes, you'll want to research the season, weather, and the type of water and its temperature for your chosen locale. Lots of South of Sixty experts will harangue you with rumours about black flies and mosquitoes. From July to August, I've never been bothered by them, but make sure you take repellent for the few pesky ones. I wish I could say that those monster blood suckers on the prairies where I've had worse experiences than North of Sixty would succumb to repellent! And forget the makeup—besides bug spray and sunscreen, all you need is tinted lip gloss, a moisturizer, and mascara, along with lots of little tubes of lotion for those daily adventures on the water. Sun, wind, and water dry you up!

What to take? Remember the Girl Guide motto: Be Prepared. Take the advice of the outfitter or lodge owner as their list is based on experience for their area, then use your discretion. It may be summer, but cold weather can blow in North of Sixty at any moment. Prepare for every kind of weather the area receives because wet and cold are not comfortable—and no one's taking you back to the lodge, Princess. Unlike our first trips North of Sixty when bulk and weight provided warmth but limited wind and water protection (you were doomed if you got wet), today's clothing and gear is lightweight, wind and water proof, quick drying, and even offers UV protection. I'll always remember the trip back to the lodge one day at Grizzly Creek—while the men trekked across land to meet us at the mouth of the Smith River, the guide slalomed us down the river. We rejoined the group at the bottom and raced across the lake in wind, rain, sleet, and snow without incident. What exhilaration when you're in good hands and you're warm and dry!

Even if it's in your DNA to look your best at all times, you don't need to be a fashionista or sell the farm for your wardrobe when on a trip north. Since my initial forays, I have discovered that layers are the best. Initially, I put together tank tops, long-sleeved shirts, a sweater, and my winter jacket; orange seemed a good colour in case anyone had to "find me." But over the years, as I've frequented the sporting good shops, I've found the sales replacing my "out-of-closet" clothes with fishing shirts and pants. And any sports equipment company will be happy to give you a baseball cap with their name on it because you'll get lots of glances being a woman fisherperson North of Sixty.

Don't go cheap on waders, wading boots, a fishing vest, and a lightweight, wind/waterproof fishing jacket; comfortable = warm + dry. Splurge on a pair of polarized sunglasses to protect your eyes, and be sure to bring a camera with underwater capabilities—on a lanyard because you don't want to dive for it—as fish watching is fun. And if it's been awhile since you've seen one near the surface, peering farther down into the water can give proof of the presence of fish. At least you know they're there when they won't take your fly! And I never leave without a book—there may be a day you need to "chill out" or simply escape the weather, or maybe you'll feel inclined to leave the men alone to fish.

As a "North of Sixty-er," I have been very fortunate in my lifetime to have fished with—and been taught by—the best, from my parents, to my husband, to all the folks in our experiences.

Over the years, much has changed North of Sixty, and the adventure-fishing bug has now bitten our son, a keen fly fisherman/fly tier who will notice many changes over *his* lifetime as a fisherman. And a bonus of fishing with my son? He no longer sees me as Mom, the agent on child-drowning prevention, but rather as Mom, the fly fisherwoman who is a competent, comfortable, and welcome part of the experience. But I also respect the boy-bonding experience father and son have every year; just don't leave me at home too often!

So from this woman's perspective on North of Sixty, you should get going—time's wasting. There are things to do, places to see, fun to be had, and fish to be caught. Any woman should strike at the lure of North of Sixty. Happy landings!

P.S. Remember gentlemen, "strike" can have many meanings if you leave her at home!

CHAPTER 10

SUMMARY
by Duane S. Radford

Because Ross H. Shickler was such a passionate fisherman, he wanted to share his experiences—along with those of other Arctic adventurers—of fishing for lake trout, grayling, and Arctic char in northern Canada. A trip to Canada's North Country is a life experience in itself for most people; throw in a fishing trip for ardent anglers, and it becomes a veritable dream come true. There are usually lots of fish to be caught, they're often not that hard to catch (except perhaps for Arctic char), and they'll test the skill and knowledge of itinerant anglers. To give those with this dream an illustration of what kind of journeys are available, we wanted to detail both do-it-yourself and lodge experiences, as well as offer a wealth of information on how and where to catch fish in northern Canada. We hope we've achieved that goal.

There's no question that the lure of trophy-sized fish is a major attraction in the North. According to information posted online on the Spectacular Northwest Territories website (http://spectacularnwt.com/whattodo/fishing/records), Canada's North Country boasts several all-tackle world records. Large grayling in the 3–4 pound range can be taken in the NWT, Nunavut, and the Yukon; lake trout from 40–50 pounds are caught routinely in each of these territories every year (while they might be the exception, they're not uncommon); and Arctic char up to 15 pounds are found in rivers throughout Nunavut and in parts of the NWT.

Some of the most notable angling records for northern Canada are as follows:

Arctic Grayling

> SIZE: 5 lb. 15 oz.
> LOCATION: Katseyedie River, NWT
> DATE: August 16, 1967
> BY: Jeanne Branson

The Katseyedie River flows into the north shore of Great Bear Lake, NWT, near what was once called the Branson's Lodge Outpost, where American outdoorswoman Jeanne Branson landed the record-book Arctic grayling in 1967. According to *Joe Brooks On Fishing* (2004), this fish hit a Mepps lure cast with a spinning outfit. Jeanne Branson also held title to the world-record Arctic char before it was broken by Jeffery Ward.

Lake Trout

> SIZE: 72 lb.
> LOCATION: Great Bear Lake, NWT
> DATE: July 19, 1991
> BY: Lloyd Bull

[Note: This entry date is in error. According to information in *Lake Trout: North America's Greatest Game Fish* (2001), Lloyd Bull caught this record fish on August 19, 1995.]

According to information obtained from IceShanty.com, Lloyd Bull netted his 72-lb. lake trout [mackinaw] in Great Bear Lake, NWT, in 1995. It was witnessed to have actually weighed 72.25 lbs. on a certified scale, and it taped 59 inches in length and 32 inches in girth. It is recognized as the all-tackle, world-record lake trout by the Canadian National Fish Registry, the National Fresh Water Fishing Hall of Fame, and the International Game Fish

Association. Lloyd is reported to have caught the trout while trolling with a Huskie Devle spoon with a single, barbless 10/0 hook. He was using a 30-lb. monofilament leader attached to 27-lb. lead-core line. The trophy fish was netted shortly before midnight and was apparently brought to shore, measured, weighed, photographed, and successfully revived and released. Lloyd Bull later recounted that in the three and a half hours prior to landing the record lake trout, he and his fishing partner Eddie House hooked more than 30 lake trout, weighing 18–38 lbs. The record lake trout was caught at the same end of the same reef that Bull's previous 56 1/2-lb., all-tackle record lake trout was caught. Bull claims to have hooked, but failed to land, even larger fish in Great Bear Lake.

Arctic Char

> SIZE: 32 lb. 9 oz.
> LOCATION: Tree River, Nunavut
> DATE: July 30, 1981
> BY: Jeffery Ward

Jeffery Ward's 32-lb. 9-oz. char was 40.5 inches long and caught with a Brass Buster jig on the Tree River, Nunavut, in a battle that only lasted about 15 minutes. The previous record char caught on the Arctic River, NWT, by Jeanne Branson weighed 29 lbs. 11 oz. Ms. Branson holds the record for the largest Arctic grayling. [Editor's note: the Arctic River may actually be the Arctic Red River. No reference can be found for the "Arctic" River.]

Brook Trout

> SIZE: 14 lb. 8 oz.
> LOCATION: Nipigon River, Ontario
> DATE: July, 1916
> BY: Dr. W. J. Cook

While we don't have details of Dr. Cook's catch, as an aside—and with no intention of being a braggart—co-editor Duane S. Radford broke the New York state record for brook trout three times in one week while fly fishing at Awesome Lake, Labrador, indicating just how many large brook trout are found in parts of northern Canada.

Atlantic Salmon

> SIZE: 79 lb. 2 oz.
> LOCATION: Tana River, Norway
> DATE: 1928
> BY: Henrik Henrikson

According to *Scott and Crossman* (1973), a 55-pound salmon caught in the Grand Cascapedia River, Quebec, may be a Canadian record. Sea-run salmon range from about 5–20 pounds in northern Canada.

Northern Pike

> SIZE: 55 lb. 1 oz.
> LOCATION: Germany

While the world-record Northern pike is from Germany, pike in northern Canada are huge, with some estimated to top 50 pounds in Manitoba (and likely elsewhere in many lakes and rivers in Canada's North Country), according to the Lucky Lures website (http://www.luckylures.nl/esox_lucius_record.php). Anglers can expect to catch pike in excess of 30 pounds in the NWT and Nunavut, and up to 40 pounds in the Yukon, though smaller pike are more common.

CHAPTER 10 | SUMMARY

Those who have ventured to Canada's North Country remain young at heart and count these trips among the best days of their lives. Faruk Ekich has enjoyed a remarkable 14 trips on the Coppermine River (see "The True Gems of the Coppermine River" on page 108), which speaks volumes about the grip Canada's North Country can have on some anglers. To quote Faruk, "As I reflect on my lifelong passion, fly fishing, I consider myself very fortunate—not so much in terms of the number of fish and their size, but in that I've lived in places that provided me with the best opportunities to pursue my passion of pursuing all species of the salmonid family."

Ross visited Plummer's Arctic Lodge on Great Bear Lake six times and made additional trips to the High Arctic Lodge on Victoria Island and Nueltin Lake Lodge, Nunavut. Co-editor Duane S. Radford has also made many trips to Canada's North Country: NWT (six times), Nunavut (three times), and the Yukon (ten times), and never tires of these northern journeys. As Ross wrote in his book, *Lake Trout: North America's Greatest Game Fish* (2001), the ancient Assyrians were of the belief that "The gods do not subtract from the span of a man's life the time spent in fishing."

With that assuring statement, I'd like to toast Ross for his idea of writing a book about fishing northern Canada for lake trout, grayling, and Arctic char. It's been a thrill for all of us involved to make his dream come true.

TRIBUTE

REMEMBERING ROSS H. SHICKLER

by **Michael Shickler, Suzanne Grady, and Matthew Shickler**

Ross H. Shickler, Ed.D. (1936–2013) on a Great Bear Lake fishing trip in 2006 (Photo credit Mike Shickler).

Our dad loved his family, he loved educating people, and he loved fishing in nature's pristine wilderness. He began fishing in earnest in the early 1940s as a young boy in western New York, inspired by his father Howard Shickler and grandfather, Ted Rogers, who had been fishing Canadian waters since the 1920s. The stories they told him and the experiences they shared served as a foundation for what would later become an intense desire to learn about and catch the elusive lake trout and their geographically close cousins, the grayling and Arctic char. This desire was more than fulfilled some 40 years later in Canada's Northwest Territories, where some say the fishing has remained unchanged for a thousand years. His motivation and thoughtful study on how to catch lakers was described in his first book, *Lake Trout: North America's Greatest Game Fish*, co-authored with Ed Eveland and published in 2001, for which he wrote a chapter entitled "Evolution of a Lake Trout Fisherman." Ed was his fishing buddy and colleague for over 30 years; he was an excellent fisherman, outdoorsman, and gourmet cook. More than eight years of researching, fishing, and writing preceded the publication of this book.

Dad took countless trips to Canada with friends and family as a young adult, and as his family grew, he followed his father's and grandfather's example, planning day trips and vacations around fishing locales. In the early 1970s, numerous day trips in southern California included fishing the East Fork of the San Gabriel Mountains for small brook trout. When the summer of 1972 arrived, the family—including Mike (eight), Suzanne (four), and Matt (one)—hurtled toward Big Sky, Montana, in a station wagon for the first of many two-week summer vacations between 1972 and 1984. Dad had learned that the Gallatin and Madison rivers were among the top 10 trout streams in the country (and still are), and with Big Sky ideally located on the western edge of Yellowstone National Park, it was the perfect place to make a base camp for fishing excursions.

In the 1990s and early 2000s, Dad fulfilled his lifetime dream of fishing Canada's Nueltin and Great Bear lakes, and while researching his first book, he interviewed Lloyd Bull. After the publication of the book, Lloyd invited Ross to his home in the Adirondacks for a few days of in-person interviews that Dad intended to use in a second book. They got to know each other as fellow anglers, and Lloyd urged Dad to come out to Great Bear

Lake and join a group of fishermen he invited to accompany him each summer. In 2006, Dad took Mike there for a week in August. Along with Lloyd and his wife Arlene, they occupied four of the 15 spots available at the Neiland Bay camp—a favourite on Great Bear Lake.

Lloyd was a walking legend among fishermen, and Dad and Mike had the pleasure of fishing with him one evening after dinner, just the three of them, without a guide. With the sun up until 11:00 p.m., fishing after dinner was not discouraged. Lloyd had visited Neiland Bay for more than 40 summers, and he knew the waters as well as anyone. It was amazing for Mike to see his dad humbly listen to and learn from the master fisherman. Mike learned a couple of tricks himself that evening and landed a 38-pound lake trout, the biggest fish he had caught—not only that week, but in his lifetime. He remains convinced that it was due to Lloyd's guidance that night.

Dad returned home from each fishing trip already planning the next trip back to Canada with Mike, Matt, or good friends, thinking about catching the next big lake trout. He inventoried and spread gear on the floor months in advance. His extensive pre-trip checklist included purchasing duplicated primary hardware, contacting and talking at length with the lodge owner, making deposits, booking flights, and checking and rechecking gear.

Mike and Matt frequently got phone calls from him each spring. On those occasions, he launched right into the subject of fishing with great excitement in his voice. "You know, the lake trout in Great Bear are getting hungry! They know that the summer thaw is coming, and they can't wait to feed—neither can I!" His son would respond, "Neither can I!" and that is how the conversations started. While some might have touched on other subjects typical of father-son conversations, the subject of fishing often remained the topic of discussion until the phone call ended.

In later years, Ross introduced fishing to his grandchildren, starting a tradition he hoped to continue with the oldest of

Suzanne's four daughters, Joceline. For her tenth birthday, he hired a local guide and took her out in a boat on Canyon Lake in southern California. Though Claire, the second oldest daughter, wanted to join them, she was too young and had to stay home. Ropa, as he was known to his grandchildren, promised Claire that he would take her fishing after she turned 10, and when Claire came of age, he kept his promise with Matt's help. He found the same guide and planned what would be his last fishing trip. This was March 2013, way too early in the season and well before the fishing conditions were good on that lake. No one had even seen a fish after a hard day out. But at the end of the day, rounding the backside of the lake, Claire hooked and landed a decent-sized smallmouth, and Matt commented that it was about as good a day of fishing as could be had. Claire and Matt will always remember Dad's last day fishing as a memorable one.

Ross's trips, his investment in the latest tackle and lures, and the contacts he made were all in the name of research on how and where to catch big fish. He meticulously researched, not just to understand better the art of catching lake trout, but to share the knowledge gained through a lifetime of experiences and the written accounts of other anglers in his books. Our dad was organized, thorough, and tenacious about getting information and presenting it well. Sadly, he passed before he could finish editing this book, but with the gracious help of Duane Radford, Stacey Aaronson, and Dad's wife, Merrie Lyn Shickler, it is now not only a reality, but a tribute to him and the subject that so captivated him. We hope you enjoyed it and will benefit from lessons learned.

Note: Mike and Matt plan to return to Great Bear Lake in the summer of 2017 to spread some of Ross's ashes and do a little fishing on the side.

NOTES ON SOURCES

Online sources are cited in the text. Various articles were provided by several authors who provided original copy or previously published works from major outdoor Canadian magazines. In the Further Reading section that follows, some of the books might appear dated; they are, however, the most recent publications. Thanks are due to Julie Warnock, NWT Tourism, for providing morphological information regarding Great Bear Lake and Great Slave Lake.

FOR FURTHER READING

Karas, Nick. *Brook Trout: A Thorough Look at North America's Greatest Native Trout—Its History, Biology and Angling Possibilities.* Lyons Press, 2002.

Hanks, Chris. *Fly Fishing in the Northwest Territories in Canada.* Portland: Frank Amato Publisher, 1996.

McPhail, J. D. and Lindsay, C. C. *Freshwater Fishes of Northwestern Canada and Alaska.* Bulletin 173. Fisheries Research Board of Canada, 1970.

Sedgwick, Don. *Joe Brooks on Fishing.* Lyons Press, 2004.

Scott, W. B. and Crossman, E. J. *Freshwater Fishes of Canada.* Bulletin 184 Fisheries. Research Board of Canada, Ottawa, 1973.

Shickler, Ross H. and Eveland, Edward M. *Lake Trout: North America's Greatest Game Fish.* Lanham and New York: The Derrydale Press, 2001.

Soucie, Gary. *Soucie's Field Guide of Fishing Facts.* Fireside (Reprint Edition), 2008.

2010 Recreational Fishing Survey of Canada. Published by the Department of Fisheries and Oceans Canada, 2012.

Yukon Freshwater Fishes: Yukon Wild. Published by the Government of Yukon, 2009.

ACKNOWLEDGEMENTS

Dr. Ross H. Shickler passed away on December 10, 2013, before he could publish this book, in concert with Canadian outdoorsman and author Duane S. Radford, former *Canadian Fly Fisher* magazine field editor for the North Country and Alberta North. Ross, a subscriber to this magazine, connected with Duane after reading his column and feature articles on fly fishing in northern Canada, and a long-distance collaboration ensued. After Ross's death, his wife, Merrie Lyn, and adult children, Michael, Suzanne, and Matthew, asked Duane to complete the book. Without him, Ross's dream of a collection of articles on Arctic fishing would not have come to fruition. There could not be a more fitting memorial, and for this, the family is deeply grateful.

Many thanks go to Stacey Aaronson of The Book Doctor Is In for designing the format and layout of this book and shepherding us through the publication process. Stacey has been a dream editor.

Appreciation goes to Ross's son, Michael, for creating the maps of Canada's North Country and the area known as the Ungava; his remembrances of his father, including photos; and his narrative of a night-fishing experience with Ross and Lloyd Bull.

Thanks are also due to Bob Sexton, *Outdoor Canada*'s Managing Editor, the go-to person for source information on articles and photo credits from *Outdoor Canada*, Canada's largest outdoor magazine.

ABOUT THE AUTHORS

Duane S. Radford

Duane Radford with a male Arctic char from the Tree River, Nunavut, (2008) taken from the Slippery Jack pool.

DUANE S. RADFORD is a nationally award-winning writer and photographer from Edmonton, Alberta, Canada. He is a past president of the Outdoor Writers of Canada, of which he's been a member since 1999, and currently serves as the chairman of the board of directors of the organization. He has published over 600 articles, as well as fish and wild game recipes in various magazines and newspapers in Canada and the United States. He is the author of two award-winning books: *Fish & Wild Game Recipes—Volume 1*

(2006) and *Conservation Pride and Passion—The Alberta Fish and Game Association 1908–2008* (2008), which he co-authored with Don Meredith. He also authored *The Cowboy Way* (2014), a book published by Blue Bike Publishers.

Duane was born in Blairmore, Alberta, and grew up in nearby Bellevue where he started hunting and fishing at an early age. He took his grade school in various towns in the Crowsnest Pass, finished high school in Calgary, and attended the University of Calgary and the University of Manitoba where he completed his Bachelor of Science and Master of Science degrees in zoology and biology. He is certified as a Fisheries Scientist by the American Fisheries Society, and has worked as a Fisheries Research Biologist, Regional Fisheries Biologist, Regional Director, and Fisheries Director for the Alberta Fish and Wildlife Division over a career spanning 34 years.

A recipient of the Order of the Bighorn Award—Alberta's highest award for fish and wildlife conservation—Duane currently resides in Edmonton, Alberta, where he works as a freelance writer and photographer. In addition to the Outdoor Writers of Canada, he belongs to Lone Pine Photo (a quality stock photo agency in Saskatoon, Saskatchewan), the Alberta Fish and Game Association, Edmonton Trout Fishing Club, and Trout Unlimited Canada. He is a former director and vice-president of the Edmonton Trout Fishing Club, and is an honourary life member of the Great Plains Fishery Workers Association. Duane was a field editor for the Northwest Territories, Nunavut, and Yukon, for the *Canadian Fly Fisher* magazine, and Alberta North, and he is a regular columnist in *Alberta Outdoorsmen* magazine: Fish(ing) Lines and Fish and Wild Game Recipes, from the Field to the Table.

Ross H. Shickler

Kugluktuk Inuit fishing guide, Morris Onipkak (L), and Ross with an elusive 20-pound male Arctic char in spawning colour, which was successfully released on the Tree River (2006). According to Ross's son, Mike, this was perhaps Ross's favourite catch in his fishing lifetime, which is saying a lot (Photo credit Mike Shickler).

An angler since the age of three, ROSS SHICKLER was born in Buffalo, New York, which he considered a family gateway to Canada's great angling opportunities, initially explored by his grandfather in the 1920s. He grew up on the shores of western New York's beautiful Chautauqua Lake where he honed his formative fishing skills. He later attended the Fredonia campus of the State University of New York where he obtained his bachelor's and master's degrees, majoring in science education with a minor in history. In 1983 he received a doctorate degree in educational administration from the University of Southern California. After teaching science at junior high and high school levels in the Long Beach Unified School District, he assumed administrative positions in the district.

Ross co-authored the book *Lake Trout: North America's Greatest Game Fish* (2001) with Edward M. Eveland, and was a member of the International Game Fish Association, National Fresh Water Fishing Hall of Fame, Ontario Federation of Anglers and Hunters, National Fishing Lure Collectors Club, Canada's National History Society, Catalina Island Conservancy, and the Outdoor Writers Association of America. Ross enjoyed fishing trips in Ontario and at Nueltin and Great Bear Lakes in Nunavut and the Northwest Territories, respectively, where he became hooked on fishing in The Land of the Midnight Sun, particularly for lake trout. He also fished the Coppermine River and lakes and rivers on Victoria Island in Canada's Arctic Archipelago. He always spoke very highly of his fishing trips at Nueltin Fly-In Lodges, Plummer's Arctic Lodges, and High Arctic Lodge.

www.ingramcontent.com/pod-product-compliance
Lightning Source LLC
Chambersburg PA
CBHW062109290426
44110CB00023B/2753